FROM MANY, ONE

Edward Francis Gabriele

FROM MANY, ONE

Praying Our Rich and Diverse
Cultural Heritage

AVE MARIA PRESS   Notre Dame, Indiana 46556

EDWARD FRANCIS GABRIELE received a Doctorate of Ministry from the Catholic University of America with a specialization in liturgy and spirituality. He is the author of *Prayers for Dawn and Dusk* and *Act Justly, Love Tenderly and Walk Humbly: Prayers for Peace and Justice* (both from St. Mary's Press).

© 1995 by Ave Maria Press, Inc.

All rights reserved. No part of this book may be used or reproduced in any manner whatsoever except in the case of reprints in the context of reviews, without written permission from Ave Maria Press, Notre Dame, IN 46556.

International Standard Book Number: 0-87793-565-3

Library of Congress Catalog Card Number: 95-77232

Cover and text design by Elizabeth J. French

Printed and bound in the United States of America.

DEDICATION

To the Matteo and Powers families,
and to the honor of one important companion in my spiritual life,
John Edward Neitzel,
the retired first Norbertine abbot of Daylesford Abbey.

These special friends have embraced me in complete acceptance
at the table of their love
as a singular grace and privilege
from the very heart of Jesus.

To them and to all the quiet women and men of this great nation,
who courageously spread open their tables and their homes,
their compassion, their laughter and their love,
to peoples of every persuasion
without judgment and with all acceptance
precisely because they sense in every earthly creature
the very presence of Jesus Christ.

To all these,
the daily missionaries of divine compassion and kingdom peace
in the workplace and in the home,
this book of prayer is dedicated.

May their witness of life and these prayers
be a sign of hope for lasting peace
to those in the United States
who have yet to taste
the real fruits and blessings
of equal protection, true liberty
and complete justice for all.

CONTENTS

PREFACE

Since 1985, I have found myself in the task of shaping original
poetic compositions for celebrations of a liturgical nature or
for private devotions. Prayer texts, which are essentially
pieces of poetry, are always springboards for the experience of
meeting the living God and having one's life stretched beyond
the present moment. The very nature of prayer, like the act of
being caught up in poetry or music, is a challenge.

This volume of prayers has been born from a reflection
upon the never-ending struggle of pluriform persons who
desire to make the United States their home. It is born also
from a reflection upon the sad history of bigotry and oppression which have ruined the lives of so many who have come
here hoping for justice and peace. The liberty and justice of
this nation have not been automatic gifts for anyone. Often,
liberty and justice have been won only at the price of tears
and blood. Human compassion and solidarity are unfortunately only to be found in a world where intolerance,
persecution, and human bigotry exist as well. Perhaps we are
not far from other orders of creation where the weak or the
"different" are destroyed so as to preserve the survival of the
species.

However, the human animal is distinctly different. Not
subject solely to the dictates of instinct and patterns of behav-
ior, we have the ability to reflect and evolve. Our diverse
religious beliefs have been an enormous contribution to the
ongoing conversation of human societies and cultures. Our
spiritual or religious reflections upon our very nature as
human beings have led us to insights that those who appear

different from ourselves are not necessarily the enemy. The enemy is us: in our impatience, our utilitarian individualism, our fears, our self-condemning intolerance, and our angry oppressions. The real threat to our national security oftentimes is not from without. It is in the words and fists of rage that deny human dignity, civil rights, and equal protection under the law to persons who, in the final analysis, we disenfranchise simply because we are afraid of them and because their presence demands that we alter our beliefs about what it means to be human, to be American, and to be disciples of Jesus.

Starkly, and thankfully, different from Darwinian theory, the Christian tradition itself reminds us that our "survival" is radically dependent upon the human ability to love, welcome, and raise up those who are different, or weak, or in need. The gospels, the message of Jesus, call us to be something quite different from other animals. We are explicitly enjoined to feed the poor, to visit those in prisons, to clothe the naked, to love those most disenfranchised. These are the activities which signal our choice for the final happiness of heaven, our present-life cooperation with the grace of the Holy Spirit. These constitute the real Magna Carta of God's kingdom. And yet these nonnegotiable activities of faith and life are not part of our patterns of living. We see partisans subordinate human needs to political agendas. We talk the language of justice and yet practice power politics. We indeed have much to learn from our American roots and the religious message which we say is our faith in Christ Jesus.

This volume of prayers has been composed to raise to our consciousness the divine gift of pluriformity in America in the light of Christian prayer and personal belief in Jesus Christ as our Savior. In a time when human bigotry seems to be on the rise once again, it is vitally important that the call to social justice and peace, the very heart of the message of Jesus in the gospels, be heard again in our midst. Despite the separation of church and state enshrined in the Constitution of the United States, Christians have an important civic duty to pray for and live out the message of Christ's peace in this nation. The gifts of gospel, justice, and peace are important for the public health of our sisters and brothers in this country. They are important for the health of this nation overall. Each of our citizens is always in need of hearing the inner voice of goodness calling us to make of this nation a safe and joyful home for all people, regardless of our differences. Pluriformity is not an enemy. It is the very gift and lifeblood of a nation whose citizens, with very few exceptions, trace their roots back to foreign lands and cultures.

The making of any book is not solely the work of any one individual. In the first place, I am extremely grateful to Mr. Robert Hamma, my editor from Ave Maria Press. He initiated the very idea of this work. Since 1988, Bob has followed my writing career and has always been an important supporter of my efforts. I am grateful that he brought this idea to me, that he challenged and supported me in this work, and that he has contributed so much, not only to this book, but to its more basic experience of prayer and justice. I give him thanks for his professional assistance as well as his taking the time to oversee the many and varied aspects that go into such a publication.

I have much to be grateful for in the life of my friend and colleague Stephanie Gray who often looked over my shoulder at my computer monitor encouraging me to reshape a word or to be more patient with myself. I am grateful to her for her support and care in the process of seeing the sparks of life that come when word meets world in the act of poetry and prayer. I am thankful also for the beloved memory of Louis Tesconi, Esq. and Juniper Connelly, OFM Conv. These courageous men met their personal trials and persecutions and used the energy of their experiences to establish an instrument of God's peace in the formation of Damien Ministries, a social justice community in Washington, DC that serves the needs of homeless, uninsurable AIDS patients, and their families. Such courage to go beyond the prejudices of the world and to feed the needs of the most needy is nothing short of a God-given inspiration. The spirit of Lou and Juniper were with me constantly as I sought for the right word, the most appropriate phrase or image, that final burst of energy which made for the production of these prayers and poems.

Finally, I wish to honor John Edward Neitzel, retired Norbertine abbot of Daylesford Abbey in Paoli, Pennsylvania. Years ago, he taught me that all human sins could be reduced to two: fear and anger. In composing and shaping these texts, his insight was foremost in my heart. Praying for justice and praying against prejudice demand the excruciatingly painful but necessary experience of confronting one's own prejudices and soiling one's hands in the roots of one's bigotry. In listening to the hateful voice of prejudice within myself, I heard fear and anger and came to appreciate them as the first parents of distrust which obscenely mar the beauty of the human Eden.

This book became a part of my personal journey of faith. It became a stinging reminder to myself of the hard work that is gospel living in Christ. It reminds me that, without the presence of Christ and the community of believers, the work of justice and peace, which always begins in the heart, is impossible. Perhaps it may inspire the same insight in others.

INTRODUCTION

American Pluriformity as Divine Gift: The Noble Experiment, Becoming Experience

All human communities and all individuals have their myths: those powerful — almost subconscious — stories, symbols, images, and metaphors of the heart which arise from one's experience, give shape and progress to one's life, and reveal to others the depths of a person's identity and meaning. Like every other culture, the United States has its myths, its dynamic symbols and images that shape and reveal the meaning of the nation. If we were to analyze all the metaphors which express our national identity and meaning, they would reveal that we are far from a political entity, a "thing." Rather, the United States itself is a kind of collective or communal "who." Probably more than any of the other myths and symbols which express the United States' identity and mission, the primordial metaphor of the Thanksgiving Feast expresses much of what we are about as a national "who" and one member of the global village.

People from vastly different cultures, races, social structures, tribal experiences, economic systems, religious beliefs, ethical and familial mores have always come together in this nation seeking to share and receive the exquisite gifts of a fuller life, freedom from fearful persecution, and freedom for human community. In the seventeenth century, pilgrims, arriving here because their civil and human rights had been denied by authorities whose phobias persecuted them for "being different," had experienced the challenges of life in a new land, in a new hemisphere. The Native Dwellers and Resident Owners of this land, putting aside what would be their natural fears of the pilgrim-strangers, shared with them food and the beginnings of potential friendship. All sat down at table. Disparate persons shared life and food and goodness. For one brief moment in history, it was possible for culturally diverse people to come together in peace, to help one another, to build a mutually respectful and enriching community. The American metaphor of the melting pot was born. A dream glimmered into reality.

That first Thanksgiving is much, much more than just a children's story acted out on grade-school stages. Underneath the simple, layered joy of our Thanksgiving stories, the real history of that meal probably was filled with tensions; but the metaphor of the first Thanksgiving, with all its naiveté, has become a radical insight into the way of life for which our forebears fought, and for which we must still struggle. It is unfortunate that we seem to fight one another in our desire to make that first meal be the hallmark of the mission of this land.

The very foundation of America is not in the formation of our political institutions or in their perpetuation. The United States was an "experiment" in civil and human liberties that is ever becoming an evolving "experience." It is still "experimental," and probably, thankfully, always will be. American freedom, justice and peace necessitate struggle, revision, the search for insight and the daring of activism in the attempt to jar open the conscience of this nation to the challenges of the ever-unfolding future. Such has always been our history. From the landing of the pilgrims at Plymouth Rock, to the emancipation of the slaves by Lincoln, to the advent of women's suffrage, to the volatile cries for justice, civil and human rights by many groups in the 1960's, the "American Experiment" is captured in the experience of the common table. The table of American experience is a place of kaleido-scopic pluriformity: a place of tense welcomes, sometimes difficult conversations, and often a place where even the old-est members may have to fight for the drumstick. Such is the experience of large, extended families where those who come later are promised a full share in the struggle of the family table. The real beauty, and the real challenge, is the ability of those already at table to make room for "new company come lately."

It is patently naive for any of us to believe that the promises of the American melting pot are automatic or easily obtained. The pluriformity of this nation has not been a facile experience. We are humans. Humans are a fearful race — especially fearful of those we judge to be different and, hence, dangerous to our personal, corporate, or cultural securities. Our history itself points to the sad failures that we have known as a nation. It did not take long for the children of the Pilgrims to rob the Native Residents of their land and dignity. The earliest colonials brought with them African slaves who were beaten and treated like animals. We paranoidly corralled American citizens of Japanese descent into concentration camps in World War II suspecting them of possible disloyalty and espionage. Many immigrants to this land were ostracized, denied adequate housing and employment because of the color of their skin, their ethnic heritage, their religion or spiri-tual beliefs, their different political backgrounds, or their family structure. Women have always been denied equal rights in the home and workplace simply because of Western culture's andro-centric biases. Women and men of many dif-ferent minority persuasions of a personal nature are still looked upon with suspicion, derided, cheated of equal protec-tion under the law. Such is the inevitable danger of a system of life which is based upon majority rule and is suspicious of change, adaptation, revision, and reformation.

Tragically, it is our common experience that it takes the "majority" too long to revisit and relearn the "original innocence" of Pilgrims and Natives at table. We are not a homogenous grouping. Nor will we ever be, or should be! We are a pluriform nation whose diversity is too often not appreciated, cultivated, and honored as a God-given gift to the foundation of American life. We are a community of vastly different persons who have no right to inflict on others what we or our ancestors have suffered in the past. Prejudice is a funny thing. It always seems to be the unfortunate stepchild of folks who have lately come to freedom from their own oppression. Western culture, in its madcap and addictive adoration of power, always divides itself into "haves and have nots," putting someone, somewhere, sometime, at the bottom of the social ladder in derision and mockery and horror. As therapists often point out, "victims victimize." Perhaps the real legacy of this nation, the real message of the primordial Thanksgiving Feast, is the call for us to break the cycle of victimization. We need no more holocausts. We can never tolerate a Hitlerian holocaust of any kind in this nation. The world community cannot sustain nor tolerate another. To paraphrase the words of Pope Paul VI in his mid-60's address to the United Nations, we need to announce in deed and word to ourselves and to the whole world: "No more victims. Victims never again."

Being an American means being committed to the struggle to "sit at table." It took courage for those first pilgrims to sit at a table that seemed empty. It took quite a bit of courage to admit their fears and sorrows. It took even more courage to put aside new fears when odd looking neighbors emerged from the forest with food. It took a leap of faith to open hands and hearts to receive food, the sincerity of a human smile, and the presence of "different" people with whom to share a meal. Being seated at table with strangers is an unsettling experience — but an experience which, in the biblical tradition, is necessary. The scriptures reminded the people Israel always to accept the stranger, for the stranger just might be the presence of God!

It is in the light of the biblical injunction of acceptance and welcome to the stranger that we find our need for prayer. We do not pray to change the will of God. Often, the real merit of our prayers is to assist our hearts in becoming more open to God's will, more eager to do the will of God, more courageous to put into real, moral action the activity of God as it arises from our ongoing conversion of life. Certainly, we honor the separation of church and state in our nation. However, there are mutual points of convergence and agreement in the moral or belief systems of our various religious traditions and the American experience. One of these points of convergence is the willingness to grow, to change, to evolve and mature. Relatively speaking, we are a very young nation. As a "young person," America has much to learn. The radical implications of a nation whose Statue of Liberty announces welcome to all people have yet to sink deeply within our hearts. Political action, even civil protest, cannot really change the course of human prejudice which still invades and decimates our national spirit every time the bigot dons white robes and invades the dignity of the night. Real conversion, real national maturity, can only come when political action is accompanied by the nonnegotiable activity of relentless personal conversion *from* bigotry and oppression; and courageous personal conversion to work *for* the equal rights of every woman, man, and child in this nation regardless of persuasion or category. It is "we" who put labels on differences. It is "we" who lay moral judgments on people different than ourselves. It is "we" who are the perpetuators of the ultimate human obscenity, immorality and sacrilege, namely human prejudice.

Without adult reflection or a mature examination of the quality of our relationships in this nation of diverse persons, we articulate culturally and personally contrived prejudices and values as if they were essentially and necessarily divine law. We have much to learn about God's will and how God's ideas are so vastly different from our perceptions about the things of heaven — even our perceptions as enshrined in the humanly conditioned language of our religious teachings. And it is God who looks upon us in our failure to uphold the rights and protection of every member of this nation, and missions us to go back again into our world: to change, to grow, to develop, to mature, to welcome and to love with all the fiery hope that brought persecuted pilgrims to a shore-line rock in search of peace and serenity.

Shortly, we will enter a new century. It seems that every time culture enters such new periods, cultural reflection increases. Rather than join with predictors of gloom and doom, perhaps the coming years of anticipation can find us reflecting more and more upon how we might make the American Dream less a nightmare and more a reality of justice for the marvelously pluriform people who inhabit our nation and who truly are our sisters and brothers in this "noble experiment becoming experience." On our knees, we need to confess our disenfranchisement of our neighbors. We need to admit and express sorrow to God and one another for the times that our slanderous words, upheld fists, political apathy, selfish voting, or perverse delight in social inequities have robbed so many people of their dignity, the gifts of peace and justice, their inalienable right to equal protection under the law, and their personal liberty in the grace of the Holy Spirit. On our knees we need to beg for the presence of Jesus in our lives — the Beloved who never hesitated to eat and drink with, and thereby to love, those that his culture told him were "unclean." Jesus resisted and preached against those distinctions. In fact, the images of his most sacred life, the gospels, make it eminently clear that Jesus found such distinctions to be sacrilegious. Each person is the temple of the Holy Spirit.

Each human being, regardless of one's differences, is the quintessential tabernacle of God in our midst. God's presence, like the colors of a prism, is manifested in glory precisely through the differences of human beings from each other. As early Christian theology taught, the glory of God indeed is the human person fully alive! This is the nonnegotiable fabric of the Christian tradition. Who are we, then, to rob the dignity of another, deny someone the right to live in this nation in equality and freedom, simply because they "house" God a bit differently than ourselves?

Today, Jesus is inviting us to table. Jesus is asking us to invite everyone from our nation to sit at table and to share the blessings of peace, of justice, of equal rights, of freedom from fear, of the joy of belonging to one another. Jesus is asking us to feed one another with the very giftedness inside ourselves which God has given to us in the pluriformity of our essential natures, backgrounds, religious beliefs, visions of the future, and life experiences. We pray that we may have the unquestioning courage to be seated at the table where our Christ invites us. Will we accept the invitation? Will we be seated in joy, or in gloom and spite? Will we open our hands and hearts to be fed and to feed one another, or will we close in upon ourselves in anger as the meal's festivity proceeds without us? Will we be instruments of God's peace in the building of this nation for future generations of pilgrims who will always journey to this land in hope? Do we have the courage? Can we make the leap of faith trusting in a God who always "knows better?" Do we have the willingness to make a thanksgiving metaphor become a life of liberty and justice for all? Can we truly become a people of a thankful and courageous table?

EDWARD FRANCIS GABRIELE
Thanksgiving Day, 1994

USING THIS TEXT

Building upon the roots of Judaism, the practice of prayer at the various hours of the day quickly became part of the regular liturgies of the early church. Prayer saw the natural rhythms of the day and night as a means of grasping the experience of life and faith in Jesus. Daily prayer eventually took the regular rhythms of the hours of the day and made them a springboard for communal prayer using the psalms, readings from the scriptures, and song. As different as the various cultures in which primitive Christianity developed, the gradual evolution of that prayer form called "The Liturgy of the Hours" (The Divine Office) took shape over many centuries. In the beginning, the "Hours" was a communal experience. It was a regular part of the day for cosmopolitan Christians as well as for early communities of monks, nuns, and hermits.

Monastic communities developed more complex and diverse forms of the Hours or Offices: making use of greater portions of the psalms, longer readings, the multiplication of many moments of prayer throughout the day and night and, eventually, elaborate ritual. The wider communities of Christians experienced the development of "Cathedral Offices" which were distinct from the monastic experience: regular use of select portions from the psalms, shorter readings, and a concentration more upon Morning Prayer (Lauds) and Evening Prayer (Vespers). Unfortunately, the Liturgy of the Hours was affected by particular historical events which made it the domain of the ordained and members of religious communities. In these years since the Second Vatican Council, the Liturgy of the Hours is being restored as a celebration of the full community of the church. In addition, it is serving as an inspiration for the development of private devotions of prayer in the contemporary era.

The following prayer services and selections draw from various aspects of the traditions of the Liturgy of the Hours. A seven day cycle of prayers has been shaped. On each day, a different grouping of American citizens is remembered. Four prayer services are chosen for each day: Morning, Midday, Evening, and Night. Each service begins with a call to prayer. At morning and evening, this is followed by a longer prayer reflecting the traditional images of the hour: praise and adoration in the morning, thanksgiving and contrition in the evening. At midday, the central image is that of fidelity to the Law of God's Word. At night, the service begins with a traditional examination of conscience.

In each service, prayer-poems are offered for use. These poems are paraphrases of psalms or canticles traditionally associated with the respective hours. Readings are chosen from the select group's spiritual patrimony as important partners for the selections of scripture that are quoted. Precisely because they constitute important universal messages in the context of this book, particular readings have been used to "stitch" the various services of prayer throughout the week: 1 Corinthians 12,13 for Evening Prayer, Martin Luther King's famous "I Have A Dream" for Night Prayer, selections from Dietrich Bonhoeffer's The Cost of Discipleship for Midday Prayer. The services also employ regularly a poem which is a paraphrase of the traditional Lord's Prayer. Night Prayer closes with a poetic interpretation of the Salve Regina. A schematic for each service is as follows:

Morning Prayer

Call to Prayer
Morning Praise
Psalm-Poem based on Psalm 63
Second Morning Psalm-Poem
Reading from the Hebrew Scriptures
Reading from the Spiritual Heritage of the Remembered
    Community
Canticle-Poem based on The Song of Zechariah
Acclamations of Praise
Prayer-Poem: The Lord's Prayer
Midday Prayer
Call to Prayer
Psalm-Poem based on Psalm 119
Reading from the Spiritual Heritage of the Remembered
    Community
Reading from The Cost of Discipleship
Prayer-Poem: The Lord's Prayer

Evening Prayer

Call to Prayer
Evening Prayer of Thanksgiving
Psalm-Poem based on Psalm 141
Second Evening Psalm-Poem
Reading from 1 Corinthians
Reading from the Spiritual Heritage of the Remembered
    Community
Canticle-Poem based on The Song of Mary
Evening Intercessions
Prayer-Poem: The Lord's Prayer

Night Prayer

Call to Prayer (Examination of Conscience)
Psalm-Poem based on Psalm 91
Reading from the First Letter of John
Reading from M. L. King's "I Have A Dream"
Canticle-Poem Based on The Canticle of Simeon
Prayer-Poem: An Anthem to Mary based on the Salve
   Regina

In the end, the construction of these times of prayer is purely a springboard offered in the spirit of the Liturgy of the Hours. In making an initial use of this text, it is recommended that one slowly progress through the various selections. However, adaptation of the materials, formats, readings, and rhythms is left to the discretion of the individuals and groups that make use of these texts. Like all other prayers, these texts are meant to serve as an impetus for believers to make their own the task of daily prayer.

Finally, these prayers are offered as a means of elevating to explicit awareness the needs we commonly have to pray for one another as diverse and gifted persons. These prayers are also meant to evoke a spirit of repentance for the sad reality of human bigotry and prejudice that mars the heritage of our nation. Christians, in this age of ecumenical outreach and social justice concerns, have an important task to pray for and with all others around us whether we share a common faith or not. It is hoped that these texts and services of prayer can move others to a deep appreciation and love of the One God who is present to us in the many riches of the pluriform community we call "America."

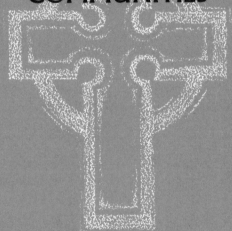

SUNDAY

ONE BODY, MANY PARTS

PRAYING WITH OUR CHRISTIAN AMERICAN COMMUNITIES

MORNING PRAYER

Call to Prayer

This is the day the Lord has made. Let us rejoice and be glad.
This is the day of victory. The day when Christ has been
raised from death. On this day the Messiah has torn down the
walls of disunity and gathered all women and men as the one,
holy People of God.

On this day, we pray for all those who call themselves
"Christian," that the God who is our cornerstone would
gather us as one church, the one Body of Christ from whom is
cast out the darkness of enmity and discord. On this day, the
sun rises on us and bids us to "Peace" with one another.

Morning Praise

God of everlasting glory,
this is the day of victory,
the day when you raised your Christ
from the dark grip of the tomb
to the bright promise and fulfillment of immortality.
All praise and glory be yours, God of life!
Loving God, in the blood of the spotless Lamb,
you gathered women and men of every age
and called them, in Christ, to be one Body.
This day we gather before you
mindful of our divisions and yet hopeful
that your Spirit may call us to a new and final day of justice
when the sword of every enmity will be put away
and we will brandish only the olive branch of peace for
    one another.
This day of the resurrection is the day of promise
for all those reborn in water and the Spirit.

And for it, we give you glory!
All praise and honor be yours, through Christ and the Spirit
  Wisdom,
forever and ever.
Amen.

Psalm 63

My soul is thirsty for you, O God.
Like a desert for water, I hunger for your love.
I look for you in the sanctuaries of the earth,
in all the secret recesses of the human heart.
More precious than bread and life is your love, your touch.
New to this day, my dry mouth gives you thirsty praise.
Every sinew and fiber of my body is filled with longing for
  your presence.
I give you praise.
I lift up my hands to you and bless your holy name.
Look toward me. Fill me with the banquet of your loving.
Make my mouth speak words of praise to you.
All through the empty night, through my tears of loneliness,
I long for your touch, your gentle presence.
Your presence invades my every thought and dream.
You are my help. I delight under the shadow of your love.
Like one who has fallen, I cling to you for my life.
You catch and lift me up to safety.
Glory be to God, to Christ and to the Spirit,
now and forever.
Amen.

Psalm 118

God is good! Give praise!
The love of God is truly without end!

All the children of Sarah and Abraham
tell of the unending love of God.
Every nation and race
tells of the unending love of God.
Every chapel and church
rings out the unending love of God.
I was surrounded by enemies and foes,
by fears and angers, resentments.
Yet God was there to give me strength
to lead me to a new day of victory.
I was thrown down in despair and left for dead.
But God did not abandon me.
Surrounded by the sting of evil,
the hand of God raised me on high.
Now the gates of a new day are thrown open to me.
I enter amid shouts of joy and praise.
This truly is God's work, blinding my blind eyes with a new
light.
Blessed is the One, the Cornerstone,
who gathers us in peace. Hosanna!
Give thanks, for our God is truly "good!"
Glory be to God, to Christ and to the Spirit,
now and forever.
Amen.

Reading I: Genesis 45: 4-5; 15

Then Joseph said to his brothers: "Come closer to me." And
they came closer. He said: "I am your brother, Joseph, whom
you sold into Egypt. And now do not be distressed, or angry
with yourselves, because you sold me here; for God sent me
before you to preserve life." And he kissed all his brothers
and wept upon them; and after that his brothers talked with
him.

Reading II: From The Decree on Ecumenism, #1, *The Documents of Vatican II*

The restoration of unity among all Christians is one of the principal concerns of the Second Vatican Council. Christ the Lord founded one Church and one Church only. However, many Christian communions present themselves to men as the true inheritors of Jesus Christ; all indeed profess to be followers of the Lord but they differ in mind and go their different ways, as if Christ himself were divided. Certainly, such division openly contradicts the will of Christ, scandalizes the world and damages the most holy cause, the preaching of the Gospel to every creature. The Lord of Ages nevertheless wisely and patiently follows out the plan of his grace on our behalf, sinners that we are. In recent times he has begun to bestow more generously upon divided Christians remorse over their divisions and longing for unity.

Gospel Canticle (based on The Song of Zechariah)

Blessed may you be, O God of Israel, our Redeemer!
Blessed is your everlasting love
which hungers for our freedom!
Blessed may you be for sending us a Savior
from the Holy House of David!
From the mouths of wandering prophets
your ancient promise of liberty was spoken.
You promised to deliver us, to save us from our enemies,
and all who wish us hatred.
You remember your covenant of peace
having sworn to set us free, to break our chains:
free to live upon this earth without fear
all the days of our lives.
O new born child, you shall be the prophet of the Lord!
You shall go before God's presence with words of promise.

You shall bring the brightness of salvation and peace;
and announce the tender mercy of God like a dawn
to all who dwell in darkness and the shadow of death,
guiding our feet into the pathways of all peace.
Glory be to God, to Christ and to the Spirit,
now and forever.
Amen.

Acclamations of Praise

This is the day on which God gathered us from death to eternal life. Gathered with all Christians and every church, we give praise to the God of all unity as we cry out: **Gracious God, we give you praise.**

♦ We worship the God who has brought us from death to life, from the tomb to eternal freedom as we pray . . .

♦ We praise the God who has fashioned us to be the one Body of Christ, proclaiming the one gospel as we pray . . .

♦ We are filled with joy at the presence of the Risen Shepherd who calls us from our divisions to a new unity of mind and heart as we pray . . .

♦ We acclaim the God who has scattered the dark night of our disunity and given us the strength of the Spirit to build again one temple of praise as we pray . . .

The Lord's Prayer (a paraphrase)

Tender God,
who lives in heaven and earth,
in human reason and passion,
you are the Holy One in our midst.
Your justice is our peace;

your peace is our hope;
your presence, our delight!
Make our hands, your hands;
our hearts, your heart;
our lives, your life!
Give us this day and always
a bread of freedom to share,
a cup of hope to pour upon the earth.
Forgive us our hatreds and walls.
Teach us to forgive the walls of others as well.
Do not permit us tests beyond our strength.
And deliver us from Evil's death-grip.
For everything above us and under us,
everything within us and without us,
must bend the knee
to the Glory of your Freedom,
the everlasting Victory
of your Justice and Peace!

MIDDAY PRAYER

Call to Prayer

This is the hour when our victory was won. This is the day of our salvation. We are caught up in the very breath and life of the God who adorns creation with the light of the divine presence in human living. We adore the majesty of the God who calls all Christians from the scandal of disunity to work for the unity of all Christians in our land and in our world. With all Christian churches and peoples of our nation, we offer our midday prayer.

Psalm 119: 1-8

Those who walk in the pathways of the blameless are truly
   "the happy."
Happy indeed are those who hold fast to God's law.
Happy are they who keep the Word
and make God's face the object of their every journey.
O God, you have commanded us to keep your laws, your
   decrees, your precepts.
Send forth your Spirit
and keep me from growing weak at noon.
Make me strong and faithful in observing your Word,
   your Law.
Then I shall not be put to shame nor disgraced
when your Word is placed before my eyes and my heart.
I give you thanks at midday and all the day.
I give you thanks with a heart filled with gratitude.
Your ordinances are my delight, my joy.
I will keep your Word.
Do not forsake me, O faithful God.
Glory be to God, to Christ and to the Spirit,
now and forever.
Amen.

Reading I: From the Decree on Ecumenism, #2, *The Documents of Vatican II*

After being lifted up on the cross and glorified, the Lord Jesus poured forth the Spirit whom he had promised, and through whom he had promised, and through whom he has called and gathered together the people of the New Covenant, which is the Church, into a unity of faith, hope and charity, as the Apostle teaches us: "There is one body and one spirit, just as you were called to the one hope of your calling; one Lord, one faith, one baptism" (Eph 4:4-5). For "all you who have been baptized into Christ have put on Christ...for you are all one in Christ Jesus" (Gal 3:27-28). It is the Holy Spirit, dwelling in those who believe and pervading and ruling over the entire Church, who brings about the wonderful communion of the faithful and joins them together so intimately in Christ that he is the principle of the Church's unity.

Reading II: From *The Cost of Discipleship*, Dietrich Bonhoeffer

"Blessed are the poor in spirit, for theirs is the kingdom of heaven." Privation is the lot of the disciples in every sphere of their lives. They are the "poor" *tout court* (Luke 6.20). They have no security, no possessions to call their own, not even a foot of earth to call their home, no earthly society to claim their absolute allegiance. Nay more, they have no spiritual power, experience or knowledge to afford them consolation or security. For his sake they have lost all. In following him they lost even their own selves and everything that could make them rich.

Now they are poor — so inexperienced, so stupid, that they have no other hope but him who called them. Jesus knows all about the others too, the representatives and preachers of the national religions, who enjoy greatness and renown, whose feet are firmly planted on the earth, who are deeply rooted in the culture and piety of the people, and molded by the spirit of the age. Yet it is not they, but the disciples who are called blessed — *theirs* is the kingdom of heaven. That kingdom dawns on *them*, the little band who for the sake of Jesus live a life of absolute renunciation and poverty. And in that very poverty they are heirs of the kingdom of heaven.

The Lord's Prayer (a paraphrase)

Tender God,
who lives in heaven and earth,
in human reason and passion,
you are the Holy One in our midst.
Your justice is our peace;
your peace is our hope;
your presence, our delight!
Make our hands, your hands;
our hearts, your heart;
our lives, your life!
Give us this day and always
a bread of freedom to share,
a cup of hope to pour upon the earth.
Forgive us our hatreds and walls.
Teach us to forgive the walls of others as well.
Do not permit us tests beyond our strength.
And deliver us from Evil's death-grip.
For everything above us and under us,
everything within us and without us,
must bend the knee
to the Glory of your Freedom,
the everlasting Victory
of your Justice and Peace!

EVENING PRAYER

Call to Prayer

This day of grace is drawing to a close. The course of the sun is giving to the coming of the night. Yet, our hearts do not fear. The lamp of Christ burns brightly in our midst. Like the two disciples on the road to Emmaus, we beg the Lord to stay with us. At this evening hour, we pray for all those who call themselves "Christian." We pray for an end to the divisions in the Body of Christ and we pray for the courage and strength that our every effort may herald the coming of a new unity of peace and charity for every Christian communion.

Evening Thanksgiving

Blessed are you, God of all the Ages!
At the beginning of time, you fashioned us in harmony
and gave us to one another as companions on our pilgrim
    way.
You did not desire us to walk this life alone.
You called us to live that same depth of love
which you have within your own self.
In the fullness of time,
you walked among us in Jesus.
This Jesus upon the cross opened his side for us
and we were given birth as a new communion in water and
    the Spirit.
One mind and one heart into you,
we took the first steps of discipleship treasuring our unity.
Yet human frailty and the temptation of power eroded our
    resistance
and led us to fracture the Body of Christ in jealousy and
    division.
We praise you this night for the Light of Christ which sweeps
    away our enmity.

We praise you for the Spirit who gives us courage to build
　　your church again in peace.
We praise you for Salvation which is the hope of all the world.
We praise you for our one Lord, one faith, one baptism
which alone are our bond of peace and justice.
All praise and honor be yours, through Christ and the Spirit
　　Wisdom,
forever and ever.
Amen.

Psalm 141

From the depths of my heart,
I cry out to you and call your name, O God.
Be not silent, but hear my pleas for your presence.
My prayers, like the smoke from incense,
go quickly up and search the crevices of the sky for you.
My hands, trembling with need, reach up and grope the air
　　for you.
O God, set your seal upon my mouth.
Be the guardian of my words and, deeper, the watcher of my
　　heart.
Never permit me to eat the bread of evildoers.
Never permit me — the freed slave — to put others in chains.
Make of me the instrument of your peace and forgiveness.
Let the evil strike me, I would not care.
Only keep me from walking in the way of evil.
Let my words and my prayers
be a source of freedom and healing for the many.
I turn my every thought and desire to you.
You alone are my refuge.
It is you that keeps me safe in the day of evil.
Glory be to God, to Christ and to the Spirit,
now and forever.
Amen.

Psalm 115

You are the glory of the ages!
Yours is the glory of the world!
To your name, and not to us, give full voice to "glory."
The powers and unbelievers mock your presence in our
    midst.
They look to our weak failures and wonder: "Where is this
    God of yours?"
But your thunder is in the heavens, your blazing light above
    us all.
Your ways are not our ways; your truth, above our
    wonderings.
You are the one God who is the cornerstone and unity of all
    the world.
You live despite our angers, our divisions, our wars with one
    another.
We have no need of vain idols of silver and gold
which cannot speak or move or love.
All those who trust in such things shall come to be exactly
    like them
As for us, we trust in you alone.
O children of peace, trust in God.
God alone is our unity and strength.
God does remember us beyond our wars
and bids us to deeds of peace for all the world.
May you be blessed by the God of love, who fashioned us for
    one another.
Even the silent dead join hands to praise God in the grave.
And so must we, one mind and heart
give praise to the God who has wedded us in peace.
Glory be to God, to Christ and to the Spirit,
now and forever.
Amen.

Reading I: 1 Corinthians 12: 1-3

Now concerning spiritual gifts, brothers and sisters, I do not want you to be uninformed. You know that when you were pagans, you were enticed and led astray to idols that could not speak. Therefore I want you to understand that no one speaking by the Spirit of God ever says, "Let Jesus be cursed!" and no one can say "Jesus is Lord" except by the Holy Spirit.

Reading II: From The Church in the Modern World, #40, *The Documents of Vatican II*

Proceeding from the love of the eternal Father, the Church was founded by Christ in time and gathered into one by the Holy Spirit. It has a saving and eschatological purpose which can be fully attained only in the next life. But it is now present here on earth and is composed of men; they, the members of the earthly city, are called to form the family of the children of God even in this present history of mankind and to increase it continually until the Lord comes. Made one in view of heavenly benefits and enriched by them, this family has been "constituted and organized as a society in the present world" by Christ and provided with means adapted to its visible and social union. Thus the Church, at once a "visible organization and a spiritual community," travels the same journey as all mankind and shares the same earthly lot with the world: it is to be a leaven and, as it were, the soul of human society in its renewal by Christ and transformation into the family of God.

Gospel Canticle (based on The Song of Mary)

From the depths of my very being,
my soul magnifies the goodness of our God!
God has looked upon me, a lowly servant!

For such goodness given to me,
all ages and all races will say that I am blest.
For God has done great things for me,
has given me freedom,
and raised me up into justice!
Holy is the name of the Just One!
Mercy comes from an open hand
to those who hunger for mercy's touch.
God the mighty has stretched forth an arm of love
and has lifted the lowly, scattering the proud.
God raises the downtrodden, the once powerful are no more.
God fills the starving poor, the comfortable go hungry.
God is ever mindful of the covenant with Israel,
the promise of all peace,
a promise made to Sarah, Abraham, and their children
unto the ages of ages, for every race and people.
Glory be to God, to Christ and to the Spirit,
now and forever.
Amen.

Evening Intercessions

Evening has come upon us. Conscious of our call to unity and
deeply aware of the scandal of the divisions among
Christians, we offer our needs to the God of every heart. And
so we pray: **Mercy on your people, Lord.**

♦ For the gift of salvation which is our common call to unity,
  peace, harmony and service, let us pray . . .

♦ For the rich diversity of gifts in the Christian Community,
  that they may be used for the service of the church and
  conversion of our world, let us pray . . .

♦ In repentance for the sad history of Christian divisions
  and for an end to the ways by which our actions and

words give credence to this scandal in the world, let us pray . . .

♦ For all those whose lives and witness give living testimony to the need and possibilities of true Christian unity among all the churches, let us pray . . .

♦ For all the dead, especially for all those who have given their lives for the sake of Christian unity, let us pray . . .

The Lord's Prayer (a paraphrase)

Tender God,
who lives in heaven and earth,
in human reason and passion,
you are the Holy One in our midst.
Your justice is our peace;
your peace is our hope;
your presence, our delight!
Make our hands, your hands;
our hearts, your heart;
our lives, your life!
Give us this day and always
a bread of freedom to share,
a cup of hope to pour upon the earth.
Forgive us our hatreds and walls.
Teach us to forgive the walls of others as well.
Do not permit us tests beyond our strength.
And deliver us from Evil's death-grip.
For everything above us and under us,
everything within us and without us,
must bend the knee
to the Glory of your Freedom,
the everlasting Victory
of your Justice and Peace!

NIGHT PRAYER

Call to Prayer

This day is full spent. We come to the time of our resting. This day we have prayed for and with the churches throughout the world, hoping for a new day of unity and peace within the entire Body of Christ. Conscious that our words and deeds may have given visible expression to the sad history of disunity among God's people, we pray this night in repentance for our sins and ask for the grace of conversion to overtake our weary hearts.

(Examination of Conscience)

For the scandal of disunity among all the members of the People of God, we cry out:

Lord, have mercy.

For the times when our apathy or suspicions have broken the Body of Christ, we cry out:

Christ, have mercy.

For the times when we have refused to see the presence of Christ in members of other Christian communities, we cry out:

Lord, have mercy.

And may almighty God forgive us our sins, grace us with new life, and give us a peaceful night.

Amen.

Psalm 91

Those who dwell in the shelter of the Most High
and abide in the shadow of God's wings

say to our God, "Our refuge,
our stronghold, the God in whom we trust."
God alone frees our feet from the hunter's snare.
God hides us in the wings of freedom and love.
No shadow or arrow can frighten us.
No plague or scourge can make us fear.
Thousands may fall around us.
Yet, the faithfulness of God will protect us.
God will bear us up to heaven's height and say:
"Since you cling to me in love, I will free you.
I shall protect you for you know my name.
I shall answer whenever you call upon me.
I will save you from all distress
and I will give you glory.
With length of days I will bless you.
I shall let you taste my peace and my justice."
Glory be to God, to Christ and to the Spirit,
now and forever.
Amen.

Reading I: 1 John 1: 8—2:2

If we say that we have no sin, we deceive ourselves, and the
truth is not in us. If we confess our sins, he who is faithful and
just will forgive us our sins and cleanse us from all unright-
eousness. If we say that we have not sinned, we make him a
liar, and his word is not in us.

My little children I am writing these things to you so that
you may not sin. But if anyone does sin, we have an advocate
with the Father, Jesus Christ the righteous; and he is the atoning sacrifice for our sins, and not for ours only but also for the
sins of the whole world.

Reading II: From *I Have a Dream,* Martin Luther King, Jr.

I am happy to join with you today in what will go down in history as the greatest demonstration for freedom in the history of our nation. Five score years ago, a great American, in whose symbolic shadow we stand today, signed the Emancipation Proclamation. This momentous decree came as a great beacon light of hope to millions of Negro slaves who had been seared in the flames of withering injustice. It came as a joyous daybreak to end the long night of their captivity. But one hundred years later, the Negro is still not free; one hundred years later, the life of the Negro is still sadly crippled by the manacles of segregation and the chains of discrimination; one hundred years later, the Negro lives on a lonely island of poverty in the midst of a vast ocean of material prosperity; one hundred years later, the Negro is still languishing in the corners of American society and finds himself in exile in his own land.

The Gospel Canticle (based on The Song of Simeon)

Now, O God of Justice,
you can dismiss your servant in the fullness of peace.
For my eyes have gazed upon the vision of your salvation,
the fulfillment of your promises of mercy
and the glory of your every race and nation.
Glory be to God, to Christ and to the Spirit,
now and forever.
Amen.

An Anthem to Mary, Mother of All the Earth

Holy Mother of all the earth,

yours are glad arms that gather the children of every nation.
You, our companion on the journey to freedom,
be with us this night and always.
As you stood faithfully near to the cross of your Child,
and held his broken body in your loving hands,
stand faithfully with us now at our many crosses.
Gather our broken lives.
Bear them to your beloved Jesus
who alone can make us one again!
O Clemens! O Pia! O Virgo Maria!
Pray for us, O Holy Mother of God,
that we may be made worthy of the promises of Christ.

MONDAY

JOYFUL PASSIONS, LOUD LAMENTS

PRAYING WITH OUR HISPANIC AMERICAN COMMUNITIES

MORNING PRAYER

Call to Prayer

On this day of grace, we rise from our sleep and greet the dawn filled with the blessings of new life. This day the Lord will unfold for us the mysteries of grace which call from our hearts our love, our compassion, our courage to stand close with those who are in pain. On this day we remember our Hispanic sisters and brothers whose rich heritage unlocks for us all the freedom to live and love with justice. We are grateful for the myriad ways in which their vast history increases our heritage. We acknowledge the horrors of discrimination which have been visited upon them; but in hope we pray that our communion with them can be built anew.

Morning Praise

O God, whose passion in Christ has redeemed us,
as the sun flashes across our world and brings us this new
    day,
we praise you with all the colors of the sky.
Dancing with wild abandon, our hopes run high
that our eyes may be open this day and always
to the miracles of your love in our midst.
This day we give you heartfelt praise and adoration
for the gift of Salvation which has become ours in the
    innocent blood of your Lamb.
Jesus walked in our midst
among flesh and blood, the peoples of his own time.
Consecrated by that holy presence,
the nations of our world have grown full to steward all
    creation.
And yet the temptations to power and arrogance

have led us too often to raise our hands in the horrors of
human hatred.
This day your Son of Justice breaks upon us with loud love
and deep compassion
to bid us put aside the weaponry which makes slaves of
others.
This day your Son of Peace calls us to a new passion,
a new outpouring of our own Spirit-filled works for the full
flowering of justice.
This day your Son of Compassion bids us to mourn fully with
those who suffer and to feed fully those whose bellies hunger
for bread and dignity.
All glory and honor be yours, O God of Loves and Laments!
All praise be yours, O God of the Flashing Sun and Dancing
Day!
All praise and honor be yours, through Christ and the Spirit
Wisdom,
forever and ever.
Amen.

Psalm 63

My soul is thirsty for you, O God.
Like a desert for water, I hunger for your love.
I look for you in the sanctuaries of the earth,
in all the secret recesses of the human heart.
More precious than bread and life is your love, your touch.
New to this day, my dry mouth gives you thirsty praise.
Every sinew and fiber of my body is filled with longing for
your presence.
I give you praise.
I lift up my hands to you and bless your holy name.
Look toward me. Fill me with the banquet of your loving.
Make my mouth speak words of praise to you.
All through the empty night, through my tears of loneliness,

I long for your touch, your gentle presence.
Your presence invades my every thought and dream.
You are my help. I delight under the shadow of your love.
Like one who has fallen, I cling to you for my life.
You catch and lift me up to safety.
Glory be to God, to Christ and to the Spirit,
now and forever.
Amen.

Psalm 85

Long ago, O God,
your favor walked within our garden.
Gently you called us from sin to life.
You covered over our sins and put aside all thought of anger.
Look upon us, O God. See us whose lives have no breath
    without you.
Breathe again into our clay and give us life.
Do not let us believe that your seeming silence somehow
    signals your anger.
Restore us to life and living. Look upon us in our exile and
    our suffering.
Let us know your mercy, your salvation and your help.
Indeed, we will hear what Word our God has for us,
a Word, a voice, that whispers "peace," within our midst:
Peace for those who rejoice; peace for those who suffer,
peace for all the peoples of the earth.
This is the God who stands close to us in our suffering and
    pain.
A God who never lets our lives sink into the silence
but raises them to daylight and to life.
The glory of the Lord dwells in our land
and flashes color into our ashen existence.
Fidelity and mercy kiss; peace and justice are entwined.
Like the lily of the field, faithfulness buds forth;

justice drops upon us like dew.
God, indeed, will make us prosper once again!
Glory be to God, to Christ and to the Spirit,
now and forever.
Amen.

Reading I: Exodus 15: 19-21

When the horses of Pharoah with his chariots and his chariot
drivers went into the sea, the LORD brought back the waters of
the sea upon them; but the Israelites walked through the sea
on dry ground. Then the prophet Miriam, Aaron's sister, took
a tambourine in her hand; and all the women went out after
her with tambourines and with dancing. And Miriam sang to
them: "Sing to the LORD, for he has triumphed gloriously;
horse and rider he has thrown into the sea."

Reading II: "Untitled" by Ana Iris Varas, Latin American Poet

Love
last night I forgot everything
I left for nowhere
I disappeared
and became
a little speck on the stove . . .
only the music remained,
in rhythm and you
on my mind.
I didn't exist
I'd disappeared
slipping into the sound wave
quivering in the air
trying to reach you.

Gospel Canticle (based on The Song of Zechariah)

Blessed may you be, O God of Israel, our Redeemer!
Blessed is your everlasting love
which hungers for our freedom!
Blessed may you be for sending us a Savior
from the Holy House of David!
From the mouths of wandering prophets
your ancient promise of liberty was spoken.
You promised to deliver us, to save us from our enemies,
and all who wish us hatred.
You remember your covenant of peace
having sworn to set us free, to break our chains:
free to live upon this earth without fear
all the days of our lives.
O newborn child, you shall be the prophet of the Lord!
You shall go before God's presence with words of promise.
You shall bring the brightness of salvation and peace;
and announce the tender mercy of God like a dawn
to all who dwell in darkness and the shadow of death,
guiding our feet into the pathways of all peace.
Glory be to God, to Christ and to the Spirit,
now and forever.
Amen.

Acclamations of Praise

On this day of salvation, we give God praise and adoration
for the rich heritage which is ours in our Hispanic American
sisters and brothers. Thankful for their presence in our community, and with them we cry out: **Praise to you, O God of
Life.**

♦ We worship the God who has enriched the fabric of our
   lives with the diversity of every race and culture as we
   pray . . .

- We praise the God who continually calls us to put aside the weapons of hatred and discrimination as we pray . . .

- We are filled with joy for the call of Jesus in our lives which leads us to struggle for the dignity of every human being as we pray . . .

- We adore the God who is forever building us into one, holy people forever freed of every form of human division as we pray . . .

The Lord's Prayer (a paraphase)

Tender God,
who lives in heaven and earth,
in human reason and passion,
you are the Holy One in our midst.
Your justice is our peace;
your peace is our hope;
your presence, our delight!
Make our hands, your hands;
our hearts, your heart;
our lives, your life!
Give us this day and always
a bread of freedom to share,
a cup of hope to pour upon the earth.
Forgive us our hatreds and walls.
Teach us to forgive the walls of others as well.
Do not permit us tests beyond our strength.
And deliver us from Evil's death-grip.
For everything above us and under us,
everything within us and without us,
must bend the knee
to the Glory of your Freedom,
the everlasting Victory
of your Justice and Peace!

MIDDAY PRAYER

Call to Prayer

In the midst of this day, we bring ourselves to pray for the
rich heritage of this land in which the peoples of many races
and nations have built their lives. We remember the God who
is always present to us especially in our presence to one
another. We worship the God who has brought our Hispanic
sisters and brothers to add their gifts of labor and love to the
fabric of our lives. In a spirit of gratitude for their presence,
and a spirit of repentance for the moments when they have
known discrimination from our hands, we offer our midday
prayer.

Psalm 119: 9-16

We ponder and wonder
if our youth can remain centered on your love, O God.
How else could they, save through the voice of your Word?
We seek you with every fiber of our being.
Do not let us stray from your pathways.
Keep us faithful to your promises, our hoping.
Above all else, you are blessed, O God of Life!
Teach us always the ways of your love.
With my every word, I proclaim your justice.
With my every breath, my hands work for your peace.
To do your holy will is enough for me.
All the riches of this world, all its honors,
are nothing.
Glory only comes in bearing your love to all I meet.
Give me your Spirit's hunger
to consume the words of your Law.
Let me never take delight in power or aggression,

nor in harsh words or the mockery of the poor.
Let me delight only in you.
Let me never forget your Word.
Glory be to God, to Christ and to the Spirit,
now and forever.
Amen.

Reading I: "The God of Children" by Marjorie Agosin, Latin American Poet

They undressed her and bound her
and speaking precisely as diplomats and surgeons
asked her
which God she believed in
that of the Moors or that of the Jews
head hanging and so far away
she kept saying
I believe in the God of children.

Reading II: From *The Cost of Discipleship,* Dietrich Bonhoeffer

"Blessed are they that mourn, for they shall be comforted." With
each beatitude the gulf is widened between the disciples and
the people, their call to come forth from the people becomes
increasingly manifest. By "mourning" Jesus, of course, means
doing without what the world calls peace and prosperity: He
means refusing to accommodate oneself to its standards. Such
men mourn for the world, for its guilt, its fate and its fortune.
While the world keeps holiday they stand aside, and while
the world sings, "Gather ye rosebuds while ye may," they
mourn. They see that for all the jollity on board, the ship is
beginning to sink. The world dreams of progress, of power
and of the future, but the disciples meditate on the end, the

last judgment, and the coming of the kingdom. To such heights the world cannot rise. And so the disciples are strangers in the world, unwelcome guests and disturbers of the peace. No wonder the world rejects them!

Why does the Christian Church so often have to look on from outside when the nation is celebrating? Have churchmen no understanding and sympathy for their fellow men? Have they become victims of misanthropy? Nobody loves his fellow men better than a disciple, nobody understands his fellow men better than the Christian fellowship, and that very love impels them to stand aside and mourn. It was a happy and suggestive thought of Luther to translate the Greek word here by the German *Leidtragen* (sorrow bearing). For the emphasis lies on the *bearing* of sorrow. The disciple community does not shake off sorrow as though it were no concern of its own, but willingly bears it. And in this way they show how close are the bonds which bind them to the rest of humanity. . . . The community of strangers find their comfort in the cross, they are comforted by being cast upon the place where the Comforter of Israel awaits them. Thus do they find their true home with their crucified Lord, both here and in eternity.

The Lord's Prayer (a paraphase)

Tender God,
who lives in heaven and earth,
in human reason and passion,
you are the Holy One in our midst.
Your justice is our peace;
your peace is our hope;
your presence, our delight!
Make our hands, your hands;
our hearts, your heart;
our lives, your life!
Give us this day and always

a bread of freedom to share,
a cup of hope to pour upon the earth.
Forgive us our hatreds and walls.
Teach us to forgive the walls of others as well.
Do not permit us tests beyond our strength.
And deliver us from Evil's death-grip.
For everything above us and under us,
everything within us and without us,
must bend the knee
to the Glory of your Freedom,
the everlasting Victory
of your Justice and Peace!

EVENING PRAYER

Call to Prayer

The sun is coming to its setting with a bright blaze of glory. As the evening approaches, the light of Christ is kindled in our midst. The living memory of the passion makes bright the recesses of our hearts and we burn with love for the Christ in our midst. At this evening, we give praise and reverence for Jesus who is present to us in the lives and witness of our Hispanic American sisters and brothers. They enrich our nation with fullness of their living humanity and thus speak to us of the glory of God. We pray both for and with them, grateful for their presence which gives freedom to our own humanity. We repent for the times that the hands of our world have made them the victims of human ignorance and discrimination.

Evening Thanksgiving

With the fullness of Love's Passion,
your glory shines within our midst, O God!
As evening falls upon us, we give you praise.
Your Christ, taking on the fullness of our flesh,
has walked among us
and shown us your glory in the richness of living humanity.
We give you praise for all the peoples
that come to grace this nation with the splendors of the
    rainbow,
spreading a light of loving among us which does not fade
for its source is Jesus, the Lamp of Justice.
This evening we give you praise for the freedom of our loving
and the liberty to share fully the sorrows of captives and
    slaves.

As Jesus embraces our loves and laments,
so we hear your call to follow in that same holy pathway.
This is our salvation: that the gift of your life in our midst
is sung when we share your life with one another in grieving
   and in joy.
We give you praise, O God, for the presence of those among
   us
who teach us to sing of the fullness of human passion
thus celebrating the memory of the One
whose passion is ever our hope!
All praise and honor be yours, through Christ and the Spirit
   Wisdom,
forever and ever.
Amen.

Psalm 141

From the depths of my heart,
I cry out to you and call your name, O God.
Be not silent, but hear my pleas for your presence.
My prayers, like the smoke from incense,
go quickly up and search the crevices of the sky for you.
My hands, trembling with need, reach up and grope the air
   for you.
O God, set your seal upon my mouth.
Be the guardian of my words and, deeper, the watcher of my
   heart.
Never permit me to eat the bread of evildoers.
Never permit me — the freed slave — to put others in chains.
Make of me the instrument of your peace and forgiveness.
Let the evil strike me, I would not care.
Only keep me from walking in the way of evil.
Let my words and my prayers
be a source of freedom and healing for the many.
I turn my every thought and desire to you.

You alone are my refuge.
It is you that keeps me safe in the day of evil.
Glory be to God, to Christ and to the Spirit,
now and forever.
Amen.

Psalm 45

Heart speaks to heart
the glad words of rejoicing and excitement.
A wedding is near. The day-heat of captivity has ended.
The sun has set upon the labors of injustice.
A chosen woman has been freed from her chains
and adorned in splendor and majesty, in strength and
    loveliness.
In her freedom, she is indeed the fairest of all the children of
    earth.
Her God has thundered from a high place, "I have chosen
    you;"
and has raised her up to her ancient dignity.
Like a warrior-maiden of old, she has a sword buckled at her
    side.
She is robed in wool as with the brightness of salvation.
Armed with arrows of justice and a skin-shield of peace,
she goes forth vindicated, among friends, to her wedding
    feast.
From the rain forests of her forebears,
she comes anointed high above all the daughters of the world.
No more sackcloth and ashes, no longer unnamed.
Nations see her glory. She is called "Holy" once again.
Leaving all behind, she inherits everything.
With strings and pipes her village-song of justice is struck up.
Her song is the song of a people yearning for peace like ripe
    corn.
May her name and her justice be our hunger, our dream

coming close.
Glory be to God, to Christ and to the Spirit,
now and forever.
Amen.

Reading I: 1 Corinthians 12: 4-11

Now there are varieties of gifts, but the same Spirit; and there
are varieties of services, but the same Lord; and there are varieties of activities, but it is the same God who activates all of
them in everyone. To each is given the manifestation of the
Spirit for the common good. To one is given through the Spirit
the utterance of wisdom, and to another the utterance of
knowledge according to the same Spirit, to another faith by
the same Spirit, to another gifts of healing by the one Spirit, to
another the working of miracles, to another prophecy, to
another the discernment of spirits, to another various kinds of
tongues, to another the interpretation of tongues. All these are
activated by one and the same Spirit, who allots to each individually just as the Spirit chooses.

Reading II: "A Story" by Roberto Saballos,
Latin American Poet

This is the story of Maria Teresa
of her weary days
and her long nights
of her lone mother
and her young son
this is the story of her boredom
of her slow steps
and her black hair
her open smile
and her old-woman's hands.

This is her story
with more grief than happiness
with fewer years than sadnesses.
This is the story of her goodbye
of her farewell without farewells.

This is the story of her mother
of her useless steps
of her quiet waiting from jail to jail
from court to court
with smiling judges
who are empty-handed.

This is the story of her eyes
that peer at her hair
her clear gaze
and her strong hands
that were lost long ago
in the cold dawn
this is the story of Maria Teresa
this is the story of my people.

Gospel Canticle (based on The Song of Mary)

From the depths of my very being,
my soul magnifies the goodness of our God!
God has looked upon me, a lowly servant!
For such goodness given to me,
all ages and all races will say that I am blest.
For God has done great things for me,
has given me freedom,
and raised me up into justice!
Holy is the name of the Just One!
Mercy comes from an open hand
to those who hunger for mercy's touch.
God the mighty has stretched forth an arm of love

and has lifted the lowly, scattering the proud.
God raises the downtrodden, the once powerful are no more.
God fills the starving poor, the comfortable go hungry.
God is ever mindful of the covenant with Israel,
the promise of all peace,
a promise made to Sarah, Abraham, and their children
unto the ages of ages, for every race and people.
Glory be to God, to Christ and to the Spirit,
now and forever.
Amen.

Evening Intercessions

Daylight is swiftly drawing to a close. At this evening hour of repentance and thanksgiving we offer our prayers and needs to the God who has enriched our land with the life and witness of our Hispanic-American sisters and brothers. And so we pray: Tender God, receive our prayer.

♦   In thanksgiving to the God who has drawn many peoples into our nation for the building of the vision of true justice and peace, let us pray . . .

♦   In thanksgiving for the full richness of life and gifts which come to us in the lives of our Hispanic-American sisters and brothers, let us pray . . .

♦   For an end to the sad legacy of violence, poverty, untreated disease, despair which so often is inflicted upon the poor of our cities and our dwellings, let us pray . . .

♦   For the times that the mighty, the wealthy, and the majority of our land shattered the dreams of the poor and the minorities in our midst; for our refusal to embrace those who are different than ourselves, let us pray . . .

♦ For those who have died, especially those who suffered violent deaths at the hands of injustice, or who suffered in martyrdom for justice's sake, let us pray . . .

The Lord's Prayer (a paraphrase)

Tender God,
who lives in heaven and earth,
in human reason and passion,
you are the Holy One in our midst.
Your justice is our peace;
your peace is our hope;
your presence, our delight!
Make our hands, your hands;
our hearts, your heart;
our lives, your life!
Give us this day and always
a bread of freedom to share,
a cup of hope to pour upon the earth.
Forgive us our hatreds and walls.
Teach us to forgive the walls of others as well.
Do not permit us tests beyond our strength.
And deliver us from Evil's death-grip.
For everything above us and under us,
everything within us and without us,
must bend the knee
to the Glory of your Freedom,
the everlasting Victory
of your Justice and Peace!

NIGHT PRAYER

Call to Prayer

Our day has come to an end. We are about to take rest from our work and receive the blessings of our resting. Deep within us, however, the discord of prejudice and bigotry keeps our hearts from coming to the full measure of sleep's reward. This day, praying with our Hispanic sisters and brothers, we remember how they have been robbed of dignity, food, and homes. Sad and repentant, we bear the sins of human prejudice to the God who heals us and bids us to put our hands to the task of building a truly humane and just city.

(Examination of Conscience)

For the disease of human hatred and bigotry in our midst, we cry out:

Lord, have mercy.

For the times when we have been deaf to the cries of those beaten by human suspicions, we cry out:

Christ, have mercy.

For the times when our apathy has robbed others of their dignity, we cry out:

Lord, have mercy.

And may almighty God forgive us our sins, grace us with new life, and give us a peaceful night.

Amen.

Psalm 91

Those who dwell in the shelter of the Most High
and abide in the shadow of God's wings

say to our God, "Our refuge,
our stronghold, the God in whom we trust."
God alone frees our feet from the hunter's snare.
God hides us in the wings of freedom and love.
No shadow or arrow can frighten us.
No plague or scourge can make us fear.
Thousands may fall around us.
Yet, the faithfulness of God will protect us.
God will bear us up to heaven's height and say:
"Since you cling to me in love, I will free you.
I shall protect you for you know my name.
I shall answer whenever you call upon me.
I will save you from all distress
and I will give you glory.
With length of days I will bless you.
I shall let you taste my peace and my justice."
Glory be to God, to Christ and to the Spirit,
now and forever.
Amen.

Reading I: 1 John 2:5b-11

By this we may be sure that we are in him: whoever says, "I
abide in him," ought to walk as he walked.

Beloved, I am writing you no new commandment, but an
old commandment that you have had from the beginning; the
old commandment is the word that you have heard. Yet I am
writing you a new commandment that is true in him and in
you, because the darkness is passing away and the true light
is already shining. Whoever says, "I am in the light," while
hating a brother or sister, is still in the darkness. Whoever
loves a brother or sister lives in the light, and in such a person
there is no cause for stumbling. But whoever hates another
believer is in the darkness, walks in the darkness, and does

not know the way to go, because the darkness has brought on blindness.

Reading II: From *I Have a Dream,* Martin Luther King, Jr.

So we've come here today to dramatize a shameful condition. In a sense we've come to our nation's capital to cash a check. When the architects of our republic wrote the magnificent words of the Constitution and the Declaration of Independence, they were signing a promissory note to which every American was to fall heir. This note was the promise that all men, yes, black men as well as white men, would be guaranteed the unalienable rights of life, liberty, and the pursuit of happiness. It is obvious today that America has defaulted on this promissory note in so far as her citizens of color are concerned. Instead of honoring this sacred obligation, America has given the Negro people a bad check; a check which has come back marked "insufficient funds." We refuse to believe that there are insufficient funds in the great vaults of opportunity of this nation. And so we've come back to cash this check, a check that will give us upon demand the riches of freedom and the security of justice.

The Gospel Canticle (based on The Song of Simeon)

Now, O God of Justice,
you can dismiss your servant in the fullness of peace.
For my eyes have gazed upon the vision of your salvation,
the fulfillment of your promises of mercy
and the glory of your every race and nation.
Glory be to God, to Christ and to the Spirit,
now and forever.
Amen.

An Anthem to Mary, Mother of All the Earth

Holy Mother of all the earth,
yours are glad arms that gather the children of every nation
You, our companion on the journey to freedom,
be with us this night and always.
As you stood faithfully near to the cross of your Child,
and held his broken body in your loving hands,
stand faithfully with us now at our many crosses.
Gather our broken lives.
Bear them to your beloved Jesus
who alone can make us one again!
O Clemens! O Pia! O Virgo Maria!
Pray for us, O Holy Mother of God,
that we may be made worthy of the promises of Christ.

TUESDAY

DARK MYSTERIES, BURNING FREEDOMS

PRAYING WITH OUR AFRICAN AMERICAN COMMUNITIES

MORNING PRAYER

Call to Prayer

As the sun rises and the night gives way to morning, we lift up our lives in praise and adoration to the God who has fashioned all peoples for freedom and joy. This day we join our hearts with our sisters and brothers throughout the African-American community. In the one bond of charity, peace and hope, we pray continually to the God who has not destined us for slavery, but for liberty. May our prayers strengthen us to be a bright light to a world too enamored of the shadows of hatred and fear.

Morning Praise

God of the Everlasting Dawn,
this day we offer you our heartfelt praise and adoration.
You are the God who looked upon us in our every need
and gave to us your Sun of Justice, Jesus our Christ.
Lost, but not forgotten,
we wandered in slavery and fear,
buffeted by the terror of angry words and hands
which robbed your people of hope and freedom.
From dense jungles and cotton fields,
from ghettos and forced labor,
our servant songs reached your ears
and you gave your freedom to us in the gift of the Cross.
This day, O God, we give you praise
for the gift of the deep mysteries of human hope and freedom
which burn brilliantly in the hearts
of all those who have suffered oppression.

This day we offer you our praise
for the gift of your everlasting strength in the Holy Spirit
who urges us forward, arms linked with one another,
to herald your peace by deeds of justice.
All praise and honor be yours, through Christ and the Spirit
  Wisdom,
forever and ever.
Amen.

Psalm 63

My soul is thirsty for you, O God.
Like a desert for water, I hunger for your love.
I look for you in the sanctuaries of the earth,
in all the secret recesses of the human heart.
More precious than bread and life is your love, your touch.
New to this day, my dry mouth gives you thirsty praise.
Every sinew and fiber of my body is filled with longing for
  your presence.
I give you praise.
I lift up my hands to you and bless your holy name.
Look toward me. Fill me with the banquet of your loving.
Make my mouth speak words of praise to you.
All through the empty night, through my tears of loneliness,
I long for your touch, your gentle presence.
Your presence invades my every thought and dream.
You are my help. I delight under the shadow of your love.
Like one who has fallen, I cling to you for my life.
You catch and lift me up to safety.
Glory be to God, to Christ and to the Spirit,
now and forever.
Amen.

Psalm 42-43

Like a wild thing, panting,
I race for the streams of your love.
I crave your presence, O God.
Taunted by the proud,
my tears of longing are like food and water to me.
My heart clings to your memory,
remembering days of joyful freedom in your dwelling place.
My soul is chained in despair, waiting for you to lift me up.
Despite the mockery of the slavers, I hope in you.
Even from my silent auction block, my heart burns hopeful
    for your freedom.
Your torrents and waves sweep over me in love, touching my
    terror,
and speaking to me words of strength.
Do not forget me, O God.
Defend me and plead my case against nations that band me
    in iron.
You are my stronghold. Deliver me from the wicked and the
    deceitful.
Like a blazing flash of lightning, send forth your truth.
Tear down the altars of oppression, the haughty monuments
    of injustice.
Break through the night-clouds of hatred and bring us to your
    temple of love.
My God, My Redeemer, I raise my soul in servant-songs.
My body and soul, like instruments, make music to your
    name.
O soul of mine, lift up your head. The God of our Ancestors
    will set you free!
Glory be to God, to Christ and to the Spirit,
now and forever.
Amen.

Reading I: Isaiah 43: 1-4

But now, thus says the Lord, he who created you, O Jacob, he who formed you, O Israel: Do not fear, for I have redeemed you; I have called you by name, you are mine. When you pass through the waters, I will be with you; and through the rivers, they shall not overwhelm you; when you walk through fire, you shall not be burned, and the flame shall not consume you. For I am the Lord, your God, the Holy One of Israel, your Savior. I give Egypt as your ransom, Ethiopia and Seba in exchange for you. Because you are precious in my sight and honored, and I love you. I give people in return for you; and nations in exchange for your life.

Reading II: "Question and Answer" by Langston Hughes

Durban, Birmingham,
Cape Town, Atlanta,
Johannesburg, Watts,
The earth around
Struggling, fighting,
Dying —- for what?

A world to gain.

Groping, hoping,
Waiting — for what?

A world to gain.

Dreams kicked asunder,
Why not go under?

There's a world to gain.

But suppose I don't want it,
Why take it?

To remake it.

Gospel Canticle (based on The Song of Zechariah)

Blessed may you be, O God of Israel, our Redeemer!
Blessed is your everlasting love
which hungers for our freedom!
Blessed may you be for sending us a Savior
from the Holy House of David!
From the mouths of wandering prophets
your ancient promise of liberty was spoken.
You promised to deliver us, to save us from our enemies,
and all who wish us hatred.
You remember your covenant of peace
having sworn to set us free, to break our chains:
free to live upon this earth without fear
all the days of our lives.
O newborn child, you shall be the prophet of the Lord!
You shall go before God's presence with words of promise.
You shall bring the brightness of salvation and peace;
and announce the tender mercy of God like a dawn
to all who dwell in darkness and the shadow of death,
guiding our feet into the pathways of all peace.
Glory be to God, to Christ and to the Spirit,
now and forever.
Amen.

Acclamations of Praise

With people of every time and place, we offer God the gift of
praise as we ask that our love be made wide enough to
include women and men of every race and nation. In this
spirit, we cry out: God of life, we give you praise.

♦ We praise the God who gives us the sun to warm every
  nation and people in freedom as we pray . . .

- ♦ We worship the God who enriches the earth with the many families of the nations as we pray . . .

- ♦ We adore the God who makes the rain to refresh us in our common labors for justice and peace as we pray . . .

- ♦ We thrill at the presence of the God who calls us from our fears to make of our world one nation united by the bond of human charity as we pray . . .

The Lord's Prayer (a paraphase)

Tender God,
who lives in heaven and earth,
in human reason and passion,
you are the Holy One in our midst.
Your justice is our peace;
your peace is our hope;
your presence, our delight!
Make our hands, your hands;
our hearts, your heart;
our lives, your life!
Give us this day and always
a bread of freedom to share,
a cup of hope to pour upon the earth.
Forgive us our hatreds and walls.
Teach us to forgive the walls of others as well.
Do not permit us tests beyond our strength.
And deliver us from Evil's death-grip.
For everything above us and under us,
everything within us and without us,
must bend the knee
to the Glory of your Freedom,
the everlasting Victory
of your Justice and Peace!

MIDDAY PRAYER

Call to Prayer

At this hour, the Savior was raised upon the cross and lifted up to the God of Mercy every race and nation. We remember the holy presence of our merciful God. We adore the majesty of the God whose only law is the law of love; whose only burden is the bond of justice and peace. With our African American sisters and brothers, we offer our midday prayer.

Psalm 119: 17-24

O God, I am your servant, your servant alone.
From your mouth comes the very breath of my life.
Without you, I cannot live!
My eyes are so often blinded by the sun of anger and despair.
Send forth your noon day brightness
and scatter my dark blindness to flight.
Like a wanderer, I walk throughout the earth
in search of your truth alone, your Word.
My soul is hungry, my heart parched,
longing to hear the glad words of your Law.
There are so many proud, so many haughty hearts
who have no room for your goodness in themselves.
Relieve me from their scorn,
from their mocking lips and threatening fists.
I do your will. That is enough for me.
Even if powers should plot against me,
and the forces of this life threaten me with utter ruin,
yet I will find my delight, my joy, my balm
in the glad tidings of your decrees.
Glory be to God, to Christ and to the Spirit,
now and forever.
Amen.

Reading I: From *Dust Tracks on the Road,* Zora Neal Hurston

Well, that is the way things stand up to now. I can look back and see sharp shadows, high lights, and smudgy in-betweens. I have been in Sorrow's kitchen and licked out all the pots. Then I have stood on the peaky mountain wrapped in rainbows, with a harp and a sword in my hands. What I had to swallow in the kitchen has not made me less glad to have lived, nor made me want to low-rate the human race, nor any whole sections of it. I take no refuge from myself in bitterness. To me, bitterness is the underarm odor of wishful weakness. It is the graceless acknowledgment of defeat. I have no urge to make any concessions like that to the world as yet. I might be like that some day, but I doubt it. I am in the struggle with the sword in my hands, and I don't intend to run until you run me. So why give off the smell of something dead under the house while I am still in there tussling with my sword in my hand?

Reading II: From *The Cost of Discipleship,* Dietrich Bonhoeffer

"Blessed are the meek: for they shall inherit the earth." This community of strangers possesses no inherent right of its own to protect its members in the world, nor do they claim such rights, for they are meek, they renounce every right of their own and live for the sake of Jesus Christ. When reproached, they hold their peace; when treated with violence they endure it patiently; when men drive them from their presence, they yield their ground. They will not go to law to defend their rights, or make a scene when they suffer injustice, nor do they insist on their legal rights. They are determined to leave their rights to God alone — *non cupidi vindictae,* as the ancient Church paraphrased it. Their right is

FROM MANY, ONE

in the will of their Lord — that and no more. They show by every word and gesture that they do not belong to this earth.

Leave heaven to them, says the world in its pity, that is where they belong. But Jesus says: "They shall inherit the earth." To these, the powerless and the disenfranchised, the whole earth belongs. Those who now possess it by violence and injustice shall lose it, and those who here have utterly renounced it, who were meek to the point of the cross, shall rule the new earth.

The Lord's Prayer (a paraphase)

Tender God,
who lives in heaven and earth,
in human reason and passion,
you are the Holy One in our midst.
Your justice is our peace;
your peace is our hope;
your presence, our delight!
Make our hands, your hands;
our hearts, your heart;
our lives, your life!
Give us this day and always
a bread of freedom to share,
a cup of hope to pour upon the earth.
Forgive us our hatreds and walls.
Teach us to forgive the walls of others as well.
Do not permit us tests beyond our strength.
And deliver us from Evil's death-grip.
For everything above us and under us,
everything within us and without us,
must bend the knee
to the Glory of your Freedom,
the everlasting Victory
of your Justice and Peace!

EVENING PRAYER

Call to Prayer

As the sun fades from view and we leave behind the heat and work of the day, we draw near to our God in thanks for gifts and riches of all nations and peoples. This evening we pray for and with our sisters and brothers in the African-American communities of our nation. We ask for forgiveness for the horror of slavery that was visited upon them by our country's ancestors. We pray that the God of all hearts would bind us with them to make of us one nation, one people, proclaiming by our lives and words that the truth of Christ has set us free.

Evening Thanksgiving

O God whose Hope, like a warrior, conquers our fears,
day is drawing to a close,
and we stand at the doorway of the night.
At this evening hour,
we gather under your tender, heavy arms to give you thanks
    and praise
for the presence of Christ in our midst
as one who dispels the fear of the shades
with the bright promise of everlasting freedom and justice.
When those first friends were enslaved by fear and doubt,
Jesus came and stood in their midst.
Touching their trembling and standing close to their shaking
    hearts,
he spoke, "Peace," and gave them strength and courage,
making them to be like warriors, proud and confident in the
    Spirit
to go forth bearing the truth of your reign to every nation in
    every language.

All praise and thanks be yours, O God of Freedom,
for the gift of Jesus in our midst
whose flaming peace is our confidence and strength.
All praise and honor be yours, through Christ and the Spirit
   Wisdom,
forever and ever.
Amen.

Psalm 141

From the depths of my heart,
I cry out to you and call your name, O God.
Be not silent, but hear my pleas for your presence.
My prayers, like the smoke from incense,
go quickly up and search the crevices of the sky for you.
My hands, trembling with need, reach up and grope the air
   for you.
O God, set your seal upon my mouth.
Be the guardian of my words and, deeper, the watcher of my
   heart.
Never permit me to eat the bread of evildoers.
Never permit me —- the freed slave —- to put others in
   chains.
Make of me the instrument of your peace and forgiveness.
Let the evil strike me, I would not care.
Only keep me from walking in the way of evil.
Let my words and my prayers
be a source of freedom and healing for the many.
I turn my every thought and desire to you.
You alone are my refuge.
It is you that keeps me safe in the day of evil.
Glory be to God, to Christ and to the Spirit,
now and forever.
Amen.

Psalm 49

Hear this, peoples of the earth.
Listen to my words, every nation,
rich and poor, learned and simple, low and high alike.
My mind is full of insight, my lips with truth.
Why should I fear those who grow rich in wealth,
whose comfort and security are riches?
No one can save their own life.
The ransom of my soul from death is beyond me.
Only fools believe that riches and wealth
can stave off death's defiant presence.
For those who trust in riches and the scorn of the poor,
it is a grave that is their final inheritance.
Those who trust in themselves alone
and place the poor in chains
are like sheep being led dumb to the butcher's block.
They do not grasp the truth.
They will vanish forever with their deeds of injustice.
But I, I trust that God alone can ransom me from death and
fear;
and God will take my soul to all peace.
Then do not fear when you see others grow rich
for riches and wealth do not last beyond the grave.
A trust in riches is a lack of wisdom
and makes us like common beasts doomed to destruction.
Glory be to God, to Christ and to the Spirit,
now and forever.
Amen.

Reading I: 1 Corinthians 12: 12-14; 26

For just as the body is one and has many members, and all the
members of the body, though many, are one body, so it is with
Christ. For in the one Spirit we were all baptized into one

body — Jews or Greeks, slaves or free — and we were all
made to drink of one Spirit. Indeed, the body does not consist
of one member but of many. If one member suffers, all suffer
together with it; of one member is honored, all rejoice
together with it.

Reading II: From *A Christmas Sermon on Peace,*
Martin Luther King, Jr.

I've seen too much hate to want to hate, myself, and I've seen
hate on the faces of too many sheriffs, too many white citizens' councilors, and too many Klansmen of the South to
want to hate, myself; and every time I see it, I say to myself,
hate is too great a burden to bear. Somehow we must be able
to stand up before our most bitter opponents and say: "We
shall match your capacity to inflict suffering by our capacity
to endure suffering. We will meet your physical force with
soul force.

Do to us what you will and we will still love you. We cannot in all good conscience obey your unjust laws and abide by
the unjust system, because noncooperation with evil is as
much a moral obligation as is cooperation with good, and so
throw us in jail and we will still love you. Bomb our homes
and threaten our children, and as difficult as it is, we will still
love you. Send your hooded perpetrators of violence into our
communities at the midnight hour and drag us out on some
wayside road and leave us half-dead as you beat us, and we
will still love you. Send your propaganda agents around the
country, and make it appear that we are not fit, culturally or
otherwise, for integration, and we'll still love you. But be
assured that we'll wear you down by our capacity to suffer,
and one day we will win our freedom. We will not only win
freedom for ourselves; we will so appeal to your heart and

conscience that we will win you in the process, and our victory will be a double victory."

Gospel Canticle (based on The Song of Mary)

From the depths of my very being,
my soul magnifies the goodness of our God!
God has looked upon me, a lowly servant!
For such goodness given to me,
all ages and all races will say that I am blest.
For God has done great things for me,
has given me freedom,
and raised me up into justice!
Holy is the name of the Just One!
Mercy comes from an open hand
to those who hunger for mercy's touch.
God the mighty has stretched forth an arm of love
and has lifted the lowly, scattering the proud.
God raises the downtrodden, the once powerful are no more.
God fills the starving poor, the comfortable go hungry.
God is ever mindful of the covenant with Israel,
the promise of all peace,
a promise made to Sarah, Abraham, and their children
unto the ages of ages, for every race and people.
Glory be to God, to Christ and to the Spirit,
now and forever.
Amen.

Evening Intercessions

As the day draws to a close, we come before the God of every people and we bear the needs and intentions of the earth to the God who hears the cries of the poor. And so we pray: **God of mercy, hear our prayer.**

- For the church and our nation, that justice and peace may be the hallmark of our laws and lives, let us pray . . .

- For the many communities of our lands, that we may be brought to repentance for the times we have enslaved others or robbed them of their dignity, let us pray . . .

- For the members of the many African-American communities in our nation, that we may be made every more grateful for the rich gifts they add to our land, let us pray . . .

- For all those who suffer in our world because of hatred, discrimination, ignorance and oppression, that the Spirit of God might set them free and raise their persecutors to the Truth, let us pray . . .

- For all those who have died, especially for all those who have been killed unjustly by violence, that the tragedy of their deaths may move us to put aside the weaponry of human hatred, let us pray . . .

The Lord's Prayer (a paraphase)

Tender God,
who lives in heaven and earth,
in human reason and passion,
you are the Holy One in our midst.
Your justice is our peace;
your peace is our hope;
your presence, our delight!
Make our hands, your hands;
our hearts, your heart;
our lives, your life!
Give us this day and always
a bread of freedom to share,
a cup of hope to pour upon the earth.

Forgive us our hatreds and walls.
Teach us to forgive the walls of others as well.
Do not permit us tests beyond our strength.
And deliver us from Evil's death-grip.
For everything above us and under us,
everything within us and without us,
must bend the knee
to the Glory of your Freedom,
the everlasting Victory
of your Justice and Peace!

NIGHT PRAYER

Call to Prayer

Day has come to an end. The nighttime calls us to sleep. As we come to take rest from our labors, we ask the enlightenment of the Holy Spirit to reveal to us our sins and give us the courage for a true conversion of life. Let us call to mind our sins, especially the ways in which we have allowed hatred and discrimination to weaken the bond of charity among us.

(Examination of Conscience)

For the times when our fears have made victims of our sisters and brothers, we cry out:

Lord, have mercy.

For the times when the courage of our loving has grown cold and uncaring, we cry out:

Christ, have mercy.

For the times when our greed and selfishness have kept others in chains, we cry out:

Lord, have mercy.

And may almighty God forgive us our sins, grace us with new life and give us a peaceful night.

Amen.

Psalm 91

Those who dwell in the shelter of the Most High
and abide in the shadow of God's wings
say to our God, "Our refuge,
our stronghold, the God in whom we trust."
God alone frees our feet from the hunter's snare.

God hides us in the wings of freedom and love.
No shadow or arrow can frighten us.
No plague or scourge can make us fear.
Thousands may fall around us.
Yet, the faithfulness of God will protect us.
God will bear us up to heaven's height and say:
"Since you cling to me in love, I will free you.
I shall protect you for you know my name.
I shall answer whenever you call upon me.
I will save you from all distress
and I will give you glory.
With length of days I will bless you.
I shall let you taste my peace and my justice."
Glory be to God, to Christ and to the Spirit,
now and forever.
Amen.

Reading I: 1 John 2: 12-15, 17

I am writing to you, little children,
    because your sins are forgiven on account of his name.
I am writing to you, fathers,
    because you know him who is from the beginning.
I am writing to you, young people,
    because you have conquered the evil one.
I write to you, children,
    because you know the Father.
I write to you, fathers,
    because you know him who is from the beginning.
I write to you, young people,
    because you are strong
    and the word of God abides in you,
        and you have overcome the evil one.
Do not love the world or the things in the world.

The world and its desire are passing away, but those who do the will of God live forever.

Reading II: From *I Have a Dream* , Martin Luther King, Jr.

We have also come to this hallowed spot to remind America of the fierce urgency of now. This is no time to engage in the luxury of cooling off or to take the tranquilizing drug of gradualism. Now is the time to make real the promises of democracy; now is the time to rise from the dark and desolate valley of segregation to the sunlit path of racial justice; now is the time to lift our nation from the quicksands of racial injustice to the solid rock of brotherhood; now is the time to make justice a reality for all God's children. It would be fatal for the nation to overlook the urgency of the moment. This sweltering summer of the Negro's legitimate discontent will not pass until there is an invigorating autumn of freedom and equality. 1963 is not an end, but a beginning. And those who hope that the Negro needed to blow off steam and will now be content, will have a rude awakening if the nation returns to business as usual.

The Gospel Canticle (based on The Song of Simeon)

Now, O God of Justice,
you can dismiss your servant in the fullness of peace.
For my eyes have gazed upon the vision of your salvation,
the fulfillment of your promises of mercy
and the glory of your every race and nation.
Glory be to God, to Christ, and to the Spirit,
now and forever.
Amen.

An Anthem to Mary, Mother of All the Earth

Holy Mother of all the earth,
yours are glad arms that gather the children of every nation.
You, our companion on the journey to freedom,
be with us this night and always.
As you stood faithfully near to the cross of your Child,
and held his broken body in your loving hands,
stand faithfully with us now at our many crosses.
Gather our broken lives.
Bear them to your beloved Jesus
who alone can make us one again!
O Clemens! O Pia! O Virgo Maria!
Pray for us, O Holy Mother of God,
that we may be made worthy of the promises of Christ.

WEDNESDAY

RISING SUN, SILENT WISDOM

PRAYING WITH OUR ASIAN AMERICAN COMMUNITIES

MORNING PRAYER

Call to Prayer

With the beauty of the lotus opening before the dawn, our hearts greet the presence of this new day. As the rays of the sun warm us to the task of building the reign of God's peace and justice once again, we remember in a special way the presence of our Asian-American sisters and brothers who grace this land with gifts for all the people. Beyond the prejudice of closed minds and hearts, we are drawn in gratitude for their life and work among us. Like all others, the God of every human heart is present to us in them. This day we offer our morning prayer in adoration of the one God whose salvation is made known in the rich diversity of every woman, man, and child.

Morning Praise

With the splendor of the rainbow,
your Sun of Justice has risen in our midst, O God.
At this morning hour, opening our lives like the gentle petals
    of the lotus,
we offer you praise and adoration as a befitting gift
for the myriad wonders of salvation in our world.
From sunrise to sunset, from field and vineyard to every city,
human hearts waken to your love.
Day speaks the words of wisdom unto day.
All peoples, from the least to the greatest,
from the lands of the east to the nations of the west,
open their hearts in full-throated praise
for the gift of the Christ in our midst.
This Jesus walked among us, in the full flesh of our humanity,
and taught us the dignity of an earth fully alive, full of your
    presence.
Filled now with your promise of peace

we are joyful for the richness and gifts of all peoples
who come to our land seeking your justice and mercy.
Your promise you crown with the Blood of the Lamb;
and for this immense gift of mercy, which waters us like the
    morning dew,
we are filled with awe.
All praise and honor be yours, through Christ and the Spirit
    Wisdom,
forever and ever.
Amen.

Psalm 63

My soul is thirsty for you, O God.
Like a desert for water, I hunger for your love.
I look for you in the sanctuaries of the earth,
in all the secret recesses of the human heart.
More precious than bread and life is your love, your touch.
New to this day, my dry mouth gives you thirsty praise.
Every sinew and fiber of my body is filled with longing for
    your presence.
I give you praise.
I lift up my hands to you and bless your holy name.
Look toward me. Fill me with the banquet of your loving.
Make my mouth speak words of praise to you.
All through the empty night, through my tears of loneliness,
I long for your touch, your gentle presence.
Your presence invades my every thought and dream.
You are my help. I delight under the shadow of your love.
Like one who has fallen, I cling to you for my life.
You catch and lift me up to safety.
Glory be to God, to Christ, and to the Spirit,
now and forever.
Amen.

FROM MANY, ONE

Psalm 77

From the fields of human labor,
we raise our hands and cry out to God.
Beset on all sides by distress and confusion,
we call to the Great Lord of Heaven
whose Word is the hope of the world's temple.
So near, yet seemingly so distant,
we refuse to be consoled.
We hunger as the poor for grain and happiness.
Our hearts are never filled by the riches of this world.
Sleep escapes us. We writhe through the night.
We remember happier days and former times,
the golden age of our loving, the years long past in nostalgia.
Will the Great Lord of Heaven never walk among us again?
Will the Great Teacher no longer speak the words of life in our
midst?
Has the love of the One vanished like the morning mists?
Has our God changed, no longer caring for our needs?
But you, O Great One, never change. Your love never ceases.
What god can be equal to your might?
You have saved us and made us to grow
from sunrise to sunset, in the endless procession of the ages.
In the temple of the earth
your Voice of Wisdom rings out like bells and chimes
call us to speak your holy name.
Glory be to God, to Christ, and to the Spirit,
now and forever.
Amen.

Reading I: Isaiah 27: 2-6

On that day: a pleasant vineyard, sing about it! I, the LORD,
am its keeper; every moment I water it. I guard it night and
day so that no one can harm it; I have no wrath. If it gives me

thorns and briars, I will march to battle against it. I will burn it up. Or else let it cling to me for protection, let it make peace with me, let it make peace with me. In the days to come Jacob shall take root, Israel shall blossom and put forth shoots, and fill the whole world with fruit.

Reading II: "The Anonymous People" by Basil Fernando, Sri Lankan Poet

We
Are the anonymous people
No photos
No paintings
To record our past
Our forefathers
Collected no stamps

No public wall
Bears our name
No awards of us
In public gains
We
Are the anonymous people
Our forefathers were the same

Ages suffering
Connects us to the past
No memories of us
But our world is vast
We
Are the anonymous people
Silence is our mask.

Gospel Canticle (based on The Song of Zechariah)

Blessed may you be, O God of Israel, our Redeemer!
Blessed is your everlasting love

which hungers for our freedom!
Blessed may you be for sending us a Savior
from the Holy House of David!
From the mouths of wandering prophets
your ancient promise of liberty was spoken.
You promised to deliver us, to save us from our enemies,
and all who wish us hatred.
You remember your covenant of peace
having sworn to set us free, to break our chains:
free to live upon this earth without fear
all the days of our lives.
O newborn child, you shall be the prophet of the Lord!
You shall go before God's presence with words of promise.
You shall bring the brightness of salvation and peace;
and announce the tender mercy of God like a dawn
to all who dwell in darkness and the shadow of death,
guiding our feet into the pathways of all peace.
Glory be to God, to Christ, and to the Spirit,
now and forever.
Amen.

Acclamations of Praise

As the sun of justice has called us to a new day, we offer our
morning praise to the God who enriches our nations with
immense gifts from our sisters and brothers from eastern
lands and cultures as we pray: **Glory be to God on High.**

◆ We worship the God who has made of our nation one
melting pot in which the rich heritage of many peoples
gives hope to all the world as we pray . . .

◆ We praise the God who has brought us the deep wisdom
and joy of our Asian-American sisters and brothers as we
pray . . .

- ◆ We are filled with joy for the continuous and never-ending invitation of God to tear down the walls of hatred and oppression which stand between us as we pray . . .

- ◆ We adore the God who has called us to give proud witness to the unity and diversity of human hearts enlightened beyond the dark power of discrimination as we pray . . .

The Lord's Prayer (a paraphase)

Tender God,
who lives in heaven and earth,
in human reason and passion,
you are the Holy One in our midst.
Your justice is our peace;
your peace is our hope;
your presence, our delight!
Make our hands, your hands;
our hearts, your heart;
our lives, your life!
Give us this day and always
a bread of freedom to share,
a cup of hope to pour upon the earth.
Forgive us our hatreds and walls.
Teach us to forgive the walls of others as well.
Do not permit us tests beyond our strength.
And deliver us from Evil's death-grip.
For everything above us and under us,
everything within us and without us,
must bend the knee
to the Glory of your Freedom,
the everlasting Victory
of your Justice and Peace!

MIDDAY PRAYER

Call to Prayer

Our labor's day has reached its midpoint. Unlike the animals, we stand apart at noon and reflect upon the stretch of the sun's rays throughout the world and throughout our nation. We stand in awe of the God who is ever present to us, and of the accomplishments wrought over the centuries by the strong hands of the many. At this midday hour, we pray for and with our Asian sisters and brothers whose pilgrimage to America is filled with gifts, but too often met with silence and suspicion. That the bright sun of human loving would dispel the shadows of oppression toward our Asian-American sisters and brothers, we offer our midday prayer to the God of all the nations.

Psalm 119: 25-32

Exhausted from the sun's heat
advancing from east to west,
we lie in the dust waiting for you to revive us, O God.
Like a farmer who has fainted in a paddyfield,
we lie, unknowing, in need of you to raise us up
and breathe into us your Life.
It is your Word that gives life.
It is your Life which is our hope and light.
It is your Hope and Light which are our rest at noon.
Overpower us with the wonders of your Word.
Stop us mid track to ponder the depths of your Love.
Keep us from the word of hatred,
the fist and handcuffs of oppression.
Give us your Spirit Wisdom
whose gentle prodding moves us to choose your Truth.

Bind us to your will alone.
Anoint us with the sweet-smelling oil of gladness
and give strength to our limbs
that we may run with joy to the garden of your delights,
the paradise of your mercy.
Glory be to God, to Christ, and to the Spirit,
now and forever.
Amen.

Reading I: "I Kept Silent" by Nguyen Chi Thien, Vietnamese Poet

I kept silent when I was tortured by my enemy:
With iron and steel, soul faint in agony —
The heroic stories are for children to believe.
I kept silent because I kept telling myself:
Has anyone, who entered the jungle and who was
run over by the wild beast
Been stupid enough to open his mouth and ask for mercy?

Reading II: From *The Cost of Discipleship,* Dietrich Bonhoeffer

"Blessed are they that hunger and thirst after righteousness: for they shall be filled." Not only do the followers of Jesus renounce their rights, they *renounce their own righteousness too.* They get no praise for their achievements and sacrifices. They cannot have righteousness except by hungering and thirst for it (this applies equally to their own righteousness and to the righteousness of God on earth), always they look forward to the future righteousness of God, but they cannot establish it for themselves. Those who follow Jesus grow hungry and thirsty on the way. They are longing for the forgiveness of all sin, for

complete renewal, for the renewal too of the earth and the full establishment of God's law.

They are still involved in the world's curse, and affected by its sin. He whom they follow must die accursed on the cross, with a desperate cry for righteousness on his lips: "My God, my God, why has thou forsaken me?" But this disciple is not above his master, he follows in his steps. Happy are they who have the promise that they shall be filled, for the righteousness they receive will be no empty promise, but real satisfaction. They will eat the Bread of Life in the Messianic Feast. They are blessed because they already enjoy this bread here and now, for in their hunger they are sustained by the bread of life, the bliss of sinners.

The Lord's Prayer (a paraphase)

Tender God,
who lives in heaven and earth,
in human reason and passion,
you are the Holy One in our midst.
Your justice is our peace;
your peace is our hope;
your presence, our delight!
Make our hands, your hands;
our hearts, your heart;
our lives, your life!
Give us this day and always
a bread of freedom to share,
a cup of hope to pour upon the earth.
Forgive us our hatreds and walls.
Teach us to forgive the walls of others as well.
Do not permit us tests beyond our strength.
And deliver us from Evil's death-grip.
For everything above us and under us,
everything within us and without us,

must bend the knee
to the Glory of your Freedom,
the everlasting Victory
of your Justice and Peace!

EVENING PRAYER

Call to Prayer

Slowly, the sun is sinking in the western sky bringing to an end another day of our love and labor. Yet the coming of the night does not bring us terror. The lamp of God's silent and eternal wisdom is brought to flame and we come in prayer to an hour of hope. At this evening, we join with our Asian-American sisters and brothers, aspiring with them to that eternal day when the justice and peace of Jesus Christ will shed the light of life, liberty and the pursuit of happiness for every woman, man and child in this nation. Repentant for the times when these sisters and brothers have suffered discrimination at our hands and the hands of our nation, we ask for pardon as we give thanks for the gift of their rich heritage in our midst.

Evening Thanksgiving

O God, whose gentle hands formed the garden of our world,
at the beginning of time
you took the clay of our existence
and breathed into us the breath of your silent Wisdom
whose gentle presence shatters the deafness of human
    misunderstanding.
Before all the ages, your Wisdom decreed our salvation.
In the fullness of time,
your holy Wisdom took flesh in the womb of the woman
and she brought to birth for us
a Savior whose love graced us
with more beauty than that of moon rays on ivory.
This night and forever, we smile in the face of darkness
for burning in our midst is the brilliant Lamp of Justice
which forever robs the forces of evil
of any share in a final victory.

This Lamp, our Jesus, leads us on through night
to the bright hope of a final day of beauty and salvation's fill.
Therefore, most gracious Lord of Heaven and Earth,
from within the secret recesses of our human hearts
we bear you gifts of thanks and repentance.
All praise and honor be yours, through Christ and the Spirit
    Wisdom,
forever and ever.
Amen.

Psalm 141

From the depths of my heart,
I cry out to you and call your name, O God.
Be not silent, but hear my pleas for your presence.
My prayers, like the smoke from incense,
go quickly up and search the crevices of the sky for you.
My hands, trembling with need, reach up and grope the air
    for you.
O God, set your seal upon my mouth.
Be the guardian of my words and, deeper, the watcher of my
    heart.
Never permit me to eat the bread of evildoers.
Never permit me — the freed slave — to put others in chains.
Make of me the instrument of your peace and forgiveness.
Let the evil strike me, I would not care.
Only keep me from walking in the way of evil.
Let my words and my prayers
be a source of freedom and healing for the many.
I turn my every thought and desire to you.
You alone are my refuge.
It is you that keeps me safe in the day of evil.
Glory be to God, to Christ, and to the Spirit,
now and forever.
Amen.

Psalm 62

Fresh from the fields of our labors,
from the anguished minds of our searching,
the bright wisdom of the ages breaks upon us
that only in God is there any final "resting."
All else is like the vanishing grass and empty winds.
Only God remains: the rock, the fortress, the mighty power of
    gentle love.
The world sets upon us.
The forces of power come to our shores and would put us in
    chains.
Despite the arrogance of the proud and the hateful,
God gives rest and strength to us in times of trouble.
All the peoples of the earth
find a refuge in God.
When others come to exploit and steal,
God becomes our only possession.
In times of conflict, it is God who gives us strength to resist.
It is the power of God which takes the sting from death.
Therefore, we do not set our hearts on riches or vanities.
For to God alone belongs the power of the nations.
To God alone belongs the gifts of love for which we hunger
    and yearn.
Glory be to God, to Christ, and to the Spirit,
now and forever.
Amen.

Reading I: 1 Corinthians 12: 27-31

Now you are the body of Christ and individually members of
it. And God has appointed in the church first apostles, second
prophets, third teachers, then deeds of power, then gifts of
healing, forms of assistance, forms of leadership, various
kinds of tongues. Are all apostles? Are all prophets? Do all

possess gifts of healing? Do all speak in tongues? Do all interpret? But strive for the greater gifts. And I will show you a still more excellent way.

Reading II: "Plowing" by Yang Lian, Chinese Poet

I am a plow
I am a betrayer of cold and death
Endless fields come toward me
They carry spring's dreams
Coming toward me, the moistened moon -
My antique, exquisite body

I am grief
I hear the groans of roots being amputated
My heart is rolling and trembling
In black waves
Like a boat fighting the storm
Like a flag quietly hoisted in humiliation
I hand frozen clumps of deep earth to the sun
Making the tract claimed by loneliness and desolation
Yield a cheerful brook once again

I am serious love
I melt unlimited tenderness with an edge of steel
More sincere than an embrace and kisses
I force all wildness, poverty and hopelessness
Far away from the great land
I give my naked soul to love
Marching on forever, spreading eternal life -
Furrow upon furrow of trenches
Plot after plot of fields
Carry my longings that gradually stretch
And submerge into new green during a radiant season

Gospel Canticle (based on The Song of Mary)

From the depths of my very being,
my soul magnifies the goodness of our God!
God has looked upon me, a lowly servant!
For such goodness given to me,
all ages and all races will say that I am blest.
For God has done great things for me,
has given me freedom,
and raised me up into justice!
Holy is the name of the Just One!
Mercy comes from an open hand
to those who hunger for mercy's touch.
God the mighty has stretched forth an arm of love
and has lifted the lowly, scattering the proud.
God raises the downtrodden, the once powerful are no more.
God fills the starving poor, the comfortable go hungry.
God is ever mindful of the covenant with Israel,
the promise of all peace,
a promise made to Sarah, Abraham, and their children
unto the ages of ages, for every race and people.
Glory be to God, to Christ and to the Spirit,
now and forever.
Amen.

Evening Intercessions

The night approaches. The sun is dying in the west. From the
east a new light, the Lamp of Justice, is kindled to bring us
hope. Grateful for the presence of the light of Christ in our
midst, we give God thanks for this day and the gift of our
repentant tears for our sins, especially for the hatreds and
apathies that have allowed the poor and the immigrant to be
fed with nothing more than the bread of injustice and violence. And so we pray: **Hear our prayer, O gracious God.**

- In thanksgiving for the original vision of our American forebears that dreamt of this land as a welcome harbor for those tossed by waves of injustice and slavery, let us pray . . .

- In thanksgiving for the extraordinary gifts of gentle wisdom and steeled courage coming to us in the lives of our Asian-American sisters and brothers, let us pray . . .

- In reparation for the spirit of inhospitality among us which mars the original blessing of our nation's vision of equality, justice, and freedom for all peoples, let us pray . . .

- In repentance for the horrors of injustice and hatred perpetrated by the forces of ignorance, for a spirit of conversion to a new day of peace and equality, let us pray . . .

- For those who have given their lives that others might eat and breathe in the full dignity of a people whose name is freedom, let us pray . . .

The Lord's Prayer (a paraphase)

Tender God,
who lives in heaven and earth,
in human reason and passion,
you are the Holy One in our midst.
Your justice is our peace;
your peace is our hope;
your presence, our delight!
Make our hands, your hands;
our hearts, your heart;
our lives, your life!
Give us this day and always
a bread of freedom to share,
a cup of hope to pour upon the earth.

Forgive us our hatreds and walls.
Teach us to forgive the walls of others as well.
Do not permit us tests beyond our strength.
And deliver us from Evil's death-grip.
For everything above us and under us,
everything within us and without us,
must bend the knee
to the Glory of your Freedom,
the everlasting Victory
of your Justice and Peace!

NIGHT PRAYER

Call to Prayer

At this hour, as we take our leave of this day of grace, God gives to all the beloved in the gift of sleep. However, before retiring we bring ourselves to this moment of prayer. Trusting in the God who keeps us as the apple of the all-seeing divine eye, we acknowledge our sins, and pray for the grace of an ongoing conversion of our lives. In a particular way, we pray in repentance for the times when the sadness of human bigotry has invaded our lives by allowing our Asian-American communities to suffer violence and poverty at our hands.

(Examination of Conscience)

For the apathy which keeps us from hearing the cries of the poor, we cry out:

Lord, have mercy.

For the times when we have allowed the immigrants to be swept upon the waves of our indifference, we cry out:

Christ, have mercy.

For the times when our fears have robbed our Asian-American sisters and brothers of the justices of employment, food, housing, and human dignity, we cry out:

Lord, have mercy.

And may almighty God forgive us our sins, grace us with new life and give us a peaceful night.

Amen.

Psalm 91

Those who dwell in the shelter of the Most High
and abide in the shadow of God's wings
say to our God, "Our refuge,

our stronghold, the God in whom we trust."
God alone frees our feet from the hunter's snare.
God hides us in the wings of freedom and love.
No shadow or arrow can frighten us.
No plague or scourge can make us fear.
Thousands may fall around us.
Yet, the faithfulness of God will protect us.
God will bear us up to heaven's height and say:
"Since you cling to me in love, I will free you.
I shall protect you for you know my name.
I shall answer whenever you call upon me.
I will save you from all distress
and I will give you glory.
With length of days I will bless you.
I shall let you taste my peace and my justice."
Glory be to God, to Christ, and to the Spirit,
now and forever.
Amen.

Reading I: 1 John 2: 24-28

Let what you heard from the beginning abide in you. If what
you heard from the beginning abides in you, then you will
abide in the Son and in the Father. And this is what he has
promised us, eternal life.

I write these things to you concerning those who would
deceive you. As for you, the anointing that you received from
him abides in you, and so you do not need anyone to teach
you. But as his anointing teaches you about all things, and is
true and is not a lie, and just as it has taught you, abide in
him.

And now, little children, abide in him, so that when he is
revealed we may have confidence and not be put to shame
before him at his coming.

Reading II: From *I Have a Dream*, Martin Luther King, Jr.

Let us not seek to satisfy our thirst for freedom by drinking from the cup of bitterness and hatred. We must forever conduct our struggle on the high plane of dignity and discipline. We must not allow our creative protest to degenerate into physical violence. Again and again we must rise to the majestic heights of meeting physical force with soul force. The marvelous militancy which has engulfed the Negro community must not lead us to distrust of all white people, for many of our white brothers, as evidenced by their presence here today, have come to realize that their destiny is tied up with our destiny and they have come to realize that their freedom is inextricably bound to our freedom. This offense we share mounted to storm the battlements of injustice must be carried forth by a biracial army. We cannot walk alone. And as we walk, we must make the pledge that we shall always march ahead. We cannot turn back.

The Gospel Canticle (based on The Song of Simeon)

Now, O God of Justice,
you can dismiss your servant in the fullness of peace.
For my eyes have gazed upon the vision of your salvation,
the fulfillment of your promises of mercy
and the glory of your every race and nation.
Glory be to God, to Christ, and to the Spirit,
now and forever.
Amen.

An Anthem to Mary, Mother of All the Earth

Holy Mother of all the earth,
yours are glad arms that gather the children of every nation.
You, our companion on the journey to freedom,

be with us this night and always.
As you stood faithfully near to the cross of your Child,
and held his broken body in your loving hands,
stand faithfully with us now at our many crosses.
Gather our broken lives.
Bear them to your beloved Jesus
who alone can make us one again!
O Clemens! O Pia! O Virgo Maria!
Pray for us, O Holy Mother of God,
that we may be made worthy of the promises of Christ.

Thursday

Forest feasts, plains' chants

Praying with our native american communities

MORNING PRAYER

Call to Prayer

With the expert skill of the hunter entering the forest boundary, the daylight has come upon us and sets to flight the forces of darkness. Dawn has come. A cry goes up throughout the earth. The rhythms of daytime once again pound in our hearts and we prepare to go forth again to our labors. On this day of our salvation, we join hearts and hands with our Native American sisters and brothers who, from the beginning, tended this wide land. Heavy with the sad memory of their oppression and forced encampment, saddened by colonial power and derision, in this day and age we pray for and with these first Americans that their gifted heritage would give us all a deeper love of that Great Spirit who is the God of all peoples.

Morning Praise

God of the Everlasting Dawn,
Great Spirit whose breath gives life to all creation,
from the gentle footfalls of forest creatures
    to the sounds of ripe ears of corn bursting in the warmth
    of the sun,
we give you praise and adoration for the gift of this day.
All adoration and honor be yours, Great God of the Earth and
    Sky!
In the fullness of time, Jesus walked among us
and took the strands of our human hearts,
plaiting our lives together as a vessel of honor
in which your love would be poured without end.
Jesus prayed for us on the heights of the mountains,
joined with us to share our meals and dreams,

heard the voices of the poor for mercy,
healed the sick, brought the dead to life,
and gave all peoples the hope of everlasting justice.
With the strength of a warrior defending the boundaries of
    your love,
with the strong fire of a mother's sacrificial love for her
    children,
Jesus embraced the cross and broke open for us a peace
to which no human treaty can compare.
All glory be yours from every nation, tribe and people.
All adoration be yours from earth's villages to heaven's
    heights.
All praise and honor be yours, through Christ and the Spirit
    Wisdom,
forever and ever.
Amen.

Psalm 63

My soul is thirsty for you, O God.
Like a desert for water, I hunger for your love.
I look for you in the sanctuaries of the earth,
in all the secret recesses of the human heart.
More precious than bread and life is your love, your touch.
New to this day, my dry mouth gives you thirsty praise.
Every sinew and fiber of my body is filled with longing for
    your presence.
I give you praise.
I lift up my hands to you and bless your holy name.
Look toward me. Fill me with the banquet of your loving.
Make my mouth speak words of praise to you.
All through the empty night, through my tears of loneliness,
I long for your touch, your gentle presence.
Your presence invades my every thought and dream.
You are my help. I delight under the shadow of your love.

FROM MANY, ONE

Like one who has fallen, I cling to you for my life.
You catch me and lift me up to safety.
Glory be to God, to Christ and to the Spirit,
now and forever.
Amen.

Psalm 80

Great Leader of the Tribes of Israel, hear our cries.
Shine forth, like the sun, upon your people.
Stir up your ardor and love for us.
Come to our aid, Great God of the Earth and Sky.
Shine your Beloved Face upon us.
Water us with the dew of salvation.
O God, how long will you seem so silent?
How long will your people's plea be answered with an empty
    wind?
Our tears are our only water; our despair is our only bread.
We are the laughing stock of other nations.
They mock us and shun us in derision.
From of old, you saved your people.
You brought them out of slavery and darkness.
You bathed them in light and clean waters.
You made of them a strong nation,
    like an ancient tree that cannot be ignored.
Visit us, we implore you, O God.
Restore us to the peace which is our life.
Do not let us sit in darkness forever.
Do not let the nations mock us in arrogance.
Let your hands be upon us with salvation.
Give us your breath that we may live again.
Glory be to God, to Christ and to the Spirit,
now and forever.
Amen.

Reading I: Isaiah 41: 8-10

But you, Israel, my servant, Jacob, whom I have chosen, the offspring of Abraham, my friend; you whom I took from the ends of the earth, and called from its farthest corners, saying to you, "You are my servant. I have chosen you and not cast you off; do not fear, for I am with you, do not be afraid, for I am your God; I will strengthen you, I will help you. I will uphold you with my victorious right hand."

Reading II: "The Town Crier Calls at Day to Announce the Feast," a Poem of the Pueblo People

All people awake, open your eyes, arise,
Become children of light, vigorous, active, sprightly.
Hasten clouds from the four world quarters;
Come now in plenty, that water may be abundant when
     summer comes;
Come ice, cover the fields, that the planting may yield
     abundance,
Let all hearts be glad!
The knowing ones will assemble in four days;
They will encircle the village dancing and singing songs . . .
The moisture may come in abundance.

Gospel Canticle (based on The Song of Zechariah)

Blessed may you be, O God of Israel, our Redeemer!
Blessed is your everlasting love
which hungers for our freedom!
Blessed may you be for sending us a Savior
from the Holy House of David!
From the mouths of wandering prophets
your ancient promise of liberty was spoken.

You promised to deliver us, to save us from our enemies,
and all who wish us hatred.
You remember your covenant of peace
having sworn to set us free, to break our chains:
free to live upon this earth without fear
all the days of our lives.
O newborn child, you shall be the prophet of the Lord!
You shall go before God's presence with words of promise.
You shall bring the brightness of salvation and peace;
and announce the tender mercy of God like a dawn
to all who dwell in darkness and the shadow of death,
guiding our feet into the pathways of all peace.
Glory be to God, to Christ, and to the Spirit,
now and forever.
Amen.

Acclamations of Praise

At the start of this new day, we join with our Native American
sisters and brothers in praise of the God who gives us
strength to build a world of justice and peace as we pray: God
of peace, all praise to you.

♦ We worship the God who graced this nation with rich
   forests and fertile foods that all might eat with justice and
   peace as we pray . . .

♦ We praise the God who has gifted this nation with the rich
   heritage of our Native American sisters and brothers as
   we pray . . .

♦ We are filled with joy for those in our midst whose courageous love has called each of us beyond the sinfulness of
   hatred and prejudice as we pray . . .

♦ We adore the God who bids us put aside the weaponry of human bigotry and bids us take up the armaments of love and respect for all peoples as we pray . . .

The Lord's Prayer (a paraphase)

Tender God,
who lives in heaven and earth,
in human reason and passion,
you are the Holy One in our midst.
Your justice is our peace;
your peace is our hope;
your presence, our delight!
Make our hands, your hands;
our hearts, your heart;
our lives, your life!
Give us this day and always
a bread of freedom to share,
a cup of hope to pour upon the earth.
Forgive us our hatreds and walls.
Teach us to forgive the walls of others as well.
Do not permit us tests beyond our strength.
And deliver us from Evil's death-grip.
For everything above us and under us,
everything within us and without us,
must bend the knee
to the Glory of your Freedom,
the everlasting Victory
of your Justice and Peace!

MIDDAY PRAYER

Call to Prayer

Having climbed to the height of this day, we are caught up in
the beauty of nature and we exhale a moment of praise and
adoration to the God whose one law is that of love alone.
Remembering the One God whose gentle majesty and powerful tenderness are our life, we join this day with our Native
American sisters and brothers. Conscious that the dark forces
of power, greed, and arrogant pride robbed them of their
lands, their dignity, and their heritage, we look forward to
new opportunities to right the wrongs they have suffered. We
look to building with them a strong nation in our midst, a
nation built upon equal justice and freedom for all.

Psalm 119

Knowing full well that human laws vanish like the dew
and human statutes fail our endless quest for your Truth,
we ask only, O God, that you teach us the depths of your
    loving.
Carve again your commandments
this time, not upon stone.
This time etch them within our hearts.
Like the carver shaping wood into an instrument of music,
bend our stiff-necked pride and fears.
Carve away the knots.
Sand down our rough edges.
Fill in our furrows.
Make of us an instrument of peace
through which your Breath of Life
can make the music of the forests and plains
soothe the beast within us all.

Keep your promises to us and raise us to a noontime of
   justice.
Keep us from our hatreds and resentments.
Do not allow our discord to ruin the sweet melody of your
   creation.
We long for your Word.
In your justice, make us live in your peace.
Glory be to God, to Christ, and to the Spirit,
now and forever.
Amen.

Reading I: "Prayer to the Mountain Spirit," a Poem of the Navajo People

Lord of the Mountain,
Reared within the Mountain
Young Man, Chieftain,
hear a young man's prayer!
Hear a prayer for cleanness.
Keeper of the strong rain,
Drumming on the mountain;
Lord of the small rain
That restores the earth in newness;
Keeper of the clean rain,
Hear a prayer for wholeness.

Young Man, Chieftain,
Hear a prayer for fleetness.
Keeper of the deer's way,
Reared among the eagles,
Clear my feet of slothness.
Keeper of the paths of men,
Hear a prayer for straightness.

Hear a prayer for courage,
Lord of the thin peaks,

Reared amid the thunders;
Keeper of the headlands
Holding up the harvest,
Keeper of the strong rocks
Hear a prayer for staunchness.

Young Man, Chieftain,
Spirit of the Mountain.

Reading II: From *The Cost of Discipleship,* Dietrich Bonhoeffer

"Blessed are the merciful, for they shall obtain mercy." These men without possessions or power, these strangers on earth, these sinners, these followers of Jesus, have in their life with him *renounced their own dignity,* for they are merciful. As if their own needs and their own distress were not enough, they take upon themselves the distress and humiliation and sin of others. They have an irresistible love for the downtrodden, the sick, the wretched, the wronged, the outcast and all who are tortured with anxiety.
They go out and seek all who are enmeshed in the toils of sin and guilt. No distress is too great, no sin too appalling for their pity. If any man falls into disgrace, the merciful will sacrifice their own honor to shield him, and take his shame upon themselves. They will be found consorting with publicans and sinners, careless of the shame they incur thereby. In order that they may be merciful they cast away the most priceless treasure of human life, their personal dignity and honor. For the only honor and glory they know is the Lord's own mercy, to which alone they owe their lives. He was not ashamed of his disciples, he became the brother of mankind, and bore their shame unto the death of the cross. That is how Jesus, the crucified, was merciful. His followers owe their lives entirely to that mercy.

The Lord's Prayer (a paraphase)

Tender God,
who lives in heaven and earth,
in human reason and passion,
you are the Holy One in our midst.
Your justice is our peace;
your peace is our hope;
your presence, our delight!
Make our hands, your hands;
our hearts, your heart;
our lives, your life!
Give us this day and always
a bread of freedom to share,
a cup of hope to pour upon the earth.
Forgive us our hatreds and walls.
Teach us to forgive the walls of others as well.
Do not permit us tests beyond our strength.
And deliver us from Evil's death-grip.
For everything above us and under us,
everything within us and without us,
must bend the knee
to the Glory of your Freedom,
the everlasting Victory
of your Justice and Peace!

EVENING PRAYER

Call to Prayer

The sun is setting over the western plains and ranges. The desert lands cool to the night chill; the evening sky is pocked with the lights from cities and villages. Despite the coming of the night, our hopes do not fade. Yet there are those of our Native American sisters and brothers for whom the coming of the night is a grim reminder of darker moments when the thief that is "hatred" robbed them of their dignity.

As we come to this hour of evening prayer, filled with praise of a God whose light in Christ never fades from us, we are likewise mindful of our need to pray for all those who have been robbed of dignity, gainful work, food, and health. This night we join with them; this night we commit ourselves to be messengers of Christ's light to all who cry out from the nightmares of their darkness.

Evening Thanksgiving

O God, whose Flame of Love never grows dim,
our world is entering into the shadows of dusk.
Though the darkness around us advances across our paths,
yet our hearts do not fear.
Within our midst is your Holy Lamp of Justice,
Jesus, raised from the dead in the brilliance of your glory,
stands in our midst and, with an endless beat and chant,
stirs us to a new courage, a new hoping, a new and eternal
    anticipation.
From ancient days, our sisters and brothers tended the forests
    and the plains.
They saw within our world your presence in all creation.
Reverencing the very presence of your Word,

alive in the movements of wind and creature,
their gentle wisdom gave praise to your gifts.
This night we give you praise.
This night we are filled with remorse
for the children of our ancestors who have been robbed of
    home and dignity.
This night your Justice is kindled in our midst.
Jesus stands before us, urging us to a new baptism
of peace and equality for all.
O God of Field and Forest, we give you praise this night and
    always
for the gift of your life that moves us to embrace all creation.
All praise and thanks be yours!
All praise and honor be yours, through Christ and the Spirit
    Wisdom,
forever and ever.
Amen.

Psalm 141

From the depths of my heart,
I cry out to you and call your name, O God.
Be not silent, but hear my pleas for your presence.
My prayers, like the smoke from incense,
go quickly up and search the crevices of the sky for you.
My hands, trembling with need, reach up and grope the air
    for you.
O God, set your seal upon my mouth.
Be the guardian of my words and, deeper, the watcher of my
    heart.
Never permit me to eat the bread of evildoers.
Never permit me — the freed slave — to put others in chains.
Make of me the instrument of your peace and forgiveness.
Let the evil strike me, I would not care.
Only keep me from walking in the way of evil.

Let my words and my prayers
be a source of freedom and healing for the many.
I turn my every thought and desire to you.
You alone are my refuge.
It is you that keeps me safe in the day of evil.
Glory be to God, to Christ and to the Spirit,
now and forever.
Amen.

Psalm 72

With a crackling fire before us,
we are caught up in the sparks of your justice,
a justice that anoints leaders and prophets
whose loud cries of peace stir us a-dancing.
With them, a fire catches on the mountain tops.
A new power is in our midst,
more enduring than sun and moon and stars.
Heat courses in our veins:
the poor will be defended; the hungry, fed;
the naked, clothed; those in chains, set free!
In the days of our new leaders, justice shall flourish like the
    mighty oak.
This Just One shall endure forever, even when the lights of
    heaven fail.
All the vanities of the nations shall be as nothing.
The Just One shall see the needy and raise them to joy.
The lives of those in danger shall be rescued.
The blood of the poor no longer will mar the earth.
We shall eat of abundant corn; and drink from clear streams
    of water.
May the name of the Just One be forever blest!
Blessed be the Great One who alone has power.
Let the Glory of our God fill every nation and tribe and
    people on earth.

Glory be to God, to Christ and to the Spirit,
now and forever.
Amen.

Reading I: 1 Corinthians 13: 1-3

If I speak in the tongues of mortals and of angels, but do not
have love, I am a noisy gong or a clanging cymbal. And if I
have prophetic powers, and understand all mysteries and all
knowledge, and if I have all faith, so as to remove mountains,
but do not have love, I am nothing. If I give away all my possessions, and if I hand over my body so that I may boast, but
do not have love, I gain nothing.

Reading II: "Song of the Vision-Maker"
(Verses 1, 2, 4, 5) a Song from the Southwest

The evening glow yet lingers;
   The evening glow yet lingers,
And I sit with my gourd rattle
   Engaged in the sacred chant.
As I wave the eagle feathers
   We hear the magic sounding.

Puissant Night is shaking me
   Just as he did at the time
When I was taken up in spirit
   To the great Magician's house.

Bluebird drifted at the edge of the world,
   Drifted along upon the blue wind.
White Wind went down from his dwelling
   And raised dust upon the earth.

The moonshine abides in me;
   And soon you men and women will see

The reed that I now am blowing
  Bring the Moon down to meet me.

Gospel Canticle (based on The Song of Mary)

From the depths of my very being,
my soul magnifies the goodness of our God!
God has looked upon me, a lowly servant!
For such goodness given to me,
all ages and all races will say that I am blest.
For God has done great things for me,
has given me freedom,
and raised me up into justice!
Holy is the name of the Just One!
Mercy comes from an open hand
to those who hunger for mercy's touch.
God the mighty has stretched forth an arm of love
and has lifted the lowly, scattering the proud.
God raises the downtrodden, the once powerful are no more.
God fills the starving poor, the comfortable go hungry.
God is ever mindful of the covenant with Israel,
the promise of all peace,
a promise made to Sarah, Abraham, and their children
unto the ages of ages, for every race and people.
Glory be to God to Christ and to the Spirit,
now and forever.
Amen.

Evening Intercessions

Once again, evening has fallen. This night, filled with praise
for the gift of our salvation, we are likewise filled with words
of love and repentance for the times when our angry words
and our consuming greed have led us to make victims of our

sisters and brothers, when our selfishness has led us far away from reverencing the presence of Christ to us in all creation. Conscious that our prayers may move us to be more open to the Spirit of God's love for one another and for all people, we bear our needs to the God who sees all and sustains all that we might love all. And so we pray: Savior God, receive our prayer.

♦ In thanks for the peoples of the Americas whose hearts and minds raised ancient cities and civilizations and monuments in testimony of the ingenuity of the human spirit, let us pray . . .

♦ In thanks for the courageous witness of our Native American sisters and brothers whose lives and cries call out to us to reverence the sacredness of the earth and the divine gift of all that lives, let us pray . . .

♦ In reparation for the bigotry and hatred which led so many of our ancestors to oppress the peoples of the Americas, let us pray . . .

♦ In repentance for the times that our arrogance and pride led us to scorn the simplicity of Wisdom and the gifts of the Spirit in every woman, man, and child, let us pray . . .

♦ For our Native American sisters and brothers who died unjustly, at the hands of violence, robbed of their dignity or lonely and despairing, let us pray. . .

The Lord's Prayer (a paraphase)

Tender God,
who lives in heaven and earth,
in human reason and passion,
you are the Holy One in our midst.
Your justice is our peace;
your peace is our hope;

your presence, our delight!
Make our hands, your hands;
our hearts, your heart;
our lives, your life!
Give us this day and always
a bread of freedom to share,
a cup of hope to pour upon the earth.
Forgive us our hatreds and walls.
Teach us to forgive the walls of others as well.
Do not permit us tests beyond our strength.
And deliver us from Evil's death-grip.
For everything above us and under us,
everything within us and without us,
must bend the knee
to the Glory of your Freedom,
the everlasting Victory
of your Justice and Peace!

NIGHT PRAYER

Call to Prayer

The embers of this day have slowly died out. Now is the hour when we are called to the gift of sleep and rest from our daily work. In our hearts, we bend our knees and open before the all-knowing heart of God what we have brought to pass in these hours. Though born of love, too often we fail and refuse to love one another as sisters and brothers. Conscious of the graces and failures we have known this day, we examine our lives under the guidance of the mercy and grace of Christ.

(Examination of Conscience)

For the selfishness that keeps us from reverencing our sister earth, we cry out:

Lord, have mercy.

For the times when we have marred the beauty of our sisters and brothers by our greed, our envy, our resentments and fears, we cry out:

Christ, have mercy.

For the times when our government and leaders have not led us to treat our Native American sisters and brothers as equals with ourselves, we cry out:

Lord, have mercy.

And may almighty God forgive us our sins, grace us with new life, and give us a peaceful night.

Amen.

Psalm 91

Those who dwell in the shelter of the Most High
and abide in the shadow of God's wings
say to our God, "Our refuge,
our stronghold, the God in whom we trust."
God alone frees our feet from the hunter's snare.
God hides us in the wings of freedom and love.
No shadow or arrow can frighten us.
No plague or scourge can make us fear.
Thousands may fall around us.
Yet, the faithfulness of God will protect us.
God will bear us up to heaven's height and say:
"Since you cling to me in love, I will free you.
I shall protect you for you know my name.
I shall answer whenever you call upon me.
I will save you from all distress
and I will give you glory.
With length of days I will bless you.
I shall let you taste my peace and my justice."
Glory be to God, to Christ, and to the Spirit,
now and forever.
Amen.

Reading I: 1 John 3: 1-3

See what love the Father has given us, that we should be
called children of God; and that is what we are. The reason
the world does not know us is that it did not know him.
Beloved, we are God's children now; what we will be has not
yet been revealed. What we do know is this: when he is
revealed, we will be like him, for we will see him as he is. And
all who have this hope in him purify themselves, just as he is
pure.

Reading II: From *I Have a Dream*, Martin Luther King, Jr.

I am not unmindful that some of you have come here out of excessive trials and tribulation. Some of you have come fresh from narrow jail cells. Some of you have come from areas where your quest for freedom left you battered by the storms of persecution and staggered by the winds of police brutality. You have been the veterans of creative suffering. Continue to work with the faith that unearned suffering is redemptive. Go back to Mississippi; go back to Alabama; go back to Georgia; go back to Louisiana; go back to the slums and ghettos of the northern cities, knowing that somehow this situation can and will be changed. Let us not wallow in the valley of despair. So I say to you, my friends, that even though we must face the difficulties of today and tomorrow, I still have a dream. It is a dream deeply rooted in the American dream that one day this nation will rise up and live out the true meaning of its creed - we hold these truths to be self-evident, that all men are created equal.

The Gospel Canticle (based on The Song of Simeon)

Now, O God of Justice,
you can dismiss your servant in the fullness of peace.
For my eyes have gazed upon the vision of your salvation,
the fulfillment of your promises of mercy
and the glory of your every race and nation.
Glory be to God, to Christ and to the Spirit,
now and forever.
Amen.

An Anthem to Mary, Mother of All the Earth

Holy Mother of all the earth,
yours are glad arms that gather the children of every nation.
You, our companion on the journey to freedom,
be with us this night and always.
As you stood faithfully near to the cross of your Child,
and held his broken body in your loving hands,
stand faithfully with us now at our many crosses.
Gather our broken lives.
Bear them to your beloved Jesus
who alone can make us one again!
O Clemens! O Pia! O Virgo Maria!
Pray for us, O Holy Mother of God,
that we may be made worthy of the promises of Christ.

FRIDAY

CRESCENT MOON, TIMELESS SANDS

PRAYING WITH OUR ISLAMIC AMERICAN COMMUNITIES

MORNING PRAYER

Call to Prayer

The sun has risen upon cities and villages, upon deserts and forests, upon all the nations of the earth. This day the God of all Peoples calls us to passionate prayer and generous service for the cause of justice and peace. As we come to this new day, we remember all our sisters and brothers who call God "Allah," and mold their lives in submission to the mercy of the divine will. Born and raised in our own times and cultures, often we forget that God is present to the world in ways which are beyond our understanding and limited human knowledge.

Begging for the Wisdom of God to open our minds and see the One Truth of Heaven, like a rainbow, in the myriad colors of different cultures and races, we join with our Islamic sisters and brothers to worship with them on their holy day of prayer. As the sun calls them to remember the salvation which is theirs, may the Son of Justice grant us the courage to lay aside our fears and join with them in the search for that peace which is the only hope of all the world.

Morning Praise

O God, whose brilliant Truth scatters the darkness of
    ignorance,
we give you adoration and praise at the start of this new day.
From the beginning of time, your people often found in
    solitude
the singular place to seek your beauty and your justice.
In the desert heat of day and the crystal cold of night,
your Truth is laid naked before the human heart.
Jesus, our Messiah, went to the desert place to seek you in
    your loving.
In a first retreat of prayer and fasting,

Jesus found your courage to wrestle with the Evil One
and thereby strengthen his arms to embrace the cross for our
    salvation.
This day we remember with joy
our sisters and brothers whose ancient prophet
speaks your word from deserts to cities.
Called to a complete submission to your holy will,
their joy at your presence leads them in a holy dance
to enrich the nations with a love of your mercy and
    compassion.
This day and forever, we join with them in peace
to give you praise for your mercy
revealed in the blood of the Spotless Lamb
whose death is our life.
All adoration and praise be yours, Eternal God of every
Temple and Faith.
All praise and honor be yours, through Christ and the Spirit
    Wisdom,
forever and ever.
Amen.

Psalm 63

My soul is thirsty for you, O God.
Like a desert for water, I hunger for your love.
I look for you in the sanctuaries of the earth,
in all the secret recesses of the human heart.
More precious than bread and life is your love, your touch.
New to this day, my dry mouth gives you thirsty praise.
Every sinew and fiber of my body is filled with longing for
    your presence.
I give you praise.
I lift up my hands to you and bless your holy name.
Look toward me. Fill me with the banquet of your loving.
Make my mouth speak words of praise to you.

All through the empty night, through my tears of loneliness,
I long for your touch, your gentle presence.
Your presence invades my every thought and dream.
You are my help. I delight under the shadow of your love.
Like one who has fallen, I cling to you for my life.
You catch me and lift me up to safety.
Glory be to God, to Christ and to the Spirit,
now and forever.
Amen.

Psalm 51

Tender of All Mercies,
mercy on your people!
Look upon us with compassion.
See us in our guilt.
Do not leave us to our shame.
Let your eyes of mercy look upon us
and blot out our many sins and lacking loves.
From the chains of our despair,
raise your hand of forgiving liberty.
Raise us up and heal us.
Take our broken bones and bind them.
Give us joy that makes us dance with whirling dervishes.
Breathe your Spirit within us
and cast out the gloom that makes us tremble.
Give us strength to do your will.
Have mercy, loving God! Forget that we have strayed.
Revive us and make us live!
Set our feet to dancing and our voices to give you praise.
Make us offer you the sacrifice of loving, repentant hearts.
Let our lives give witness to your healing love.
Glory be to God, to Christ and to the Spirit,
now and forever.
Amen.

Reading I: Genesis 21: 14-18

So Abraham rose early in the morning, and took bread and a skin of water, and gave it to Hagar, putting it on her shoulder, along with the child, and sent her away. And she departed, and wandered about in the wilderness of Beersheba. When the water in the skin was gone, she cast the child under one of the bushes. Then she went and sat down opposite him a good way off, about the distance of a bow shot; for she said, "Do not let me look on the death of the child." And as she sat opposite him, she lifted up her voice and wept. And God heard the voice of the boy; and the angel of God called to Hagar from heaven, and said to her, "What troubles you, Hagar? Do not be afraid; for God has heard the voice of the boy where he is. Come, lift up the boy and hold him fast with your hand, for I will make a great nation of him."

Reading II: "Daylight" from the Koran
93: 1, 93: 6, 93: 11

By the light of day, and by the dark of night, your Lord has not forsaken you, nor does He abhor you. The life to come holds a richer prize for you than this present life. You shall be gratified with what your Lord will give you. Did He not find you an orphan and give you shelter? Did He not find you in error and guide you? Did He not find you poor and enrich you? Therefore do not wrong the orphan, nor chide away the beggar. But proclaim the goodness of your Lord.

Gospel Canticle (based on The Song of Zechariah)

Blessed may you be, O God of Israel, our Redeemer!
Blessed is your everlasting love
which hungers for our freedom!

Blessed may you be for sending us a Savior
from the Holy House of David!
From the mouths of wandering prophets
your ancient promise of liberty was spoken.
You promised to deliver us, to save us from our enemies
and all who wish us hatred.
You remember your covenant of peace
having sworn to set us free, to break our chains:
free to live upon this earth without fear
all the days of our lives.
O newborn child, you shall be the prophet of the Lord!
You shall go before God's presence with words of promise.
You shall bring the brightness of salvation and peace;
and announce the tender mercy of God like a dawn
to all who dwell in darkness and the shadow of death,
guiding our feet into the pathways of all peace.
Glory be to God, to Christ and to the Spirit,
now and forever.
Amen.

Acclamations of Praise

As daylight breaks upon us, we offer our praise and adoration
to the One God who is acclaimed as "Allah" by our Islamic
sisters and brothers as we pray: **All the earth, give praise to
God.**

♦   We worship the God who calls every nation and people to
    proclaim in their lives the final victory of justice and peace
    for all as we pray . . .

♦   We praise the God who has given the earth the beauty of
    the divine will revealed in the faith-filled witness of our
    Islamic sisters and brothers as we pray . . .

- We are filled with wonder at the presence of God whose love and truth ride swiftly across the lands and deserts of all the nations as we pray . . .

- We give praise and honor to the One God whose Truth is revealed in the love and compassion of all peoples for each other as we pray . . .

The Lord's Prayer (a paraphase)

Tender God,
who lives in heaven and earth,
in human reason and passion,
you are the Holy One in our midst.
Your justice is our peace;
your peace is our hope;
your presence, our delight!
Make our hands, your hands;
our hearts, your heart;
our lives, your life!
Give us this day and always
a bread of freedom to share,
a cup of hope to pour upon the earth.
Forgive us our hatreds and walls.
Teach us to forgive the walls of others as well.
Do not permit us tests beyond our strength.
And deliver us from Evil's death-grip.
For everything above us and under us,
everything within us and without us,
must bend the knee
to the Glory of your Freedom,
the everlasting Victory
of your Justice and Peace!

MIDDAY PRAYER

Call to Prayer

At this midday hour, we join our hands and hearts with our Islamic sisters and brothers to the One True God whom they invoke as "Allah," the Almighty yet Tender One. Grateful for their witness of compassion and care to the orphaned and the disconsolate, we remember the Holy Presence of God. We adore the Divine Majesty who sees all, who knows all, who sustains all, who loves all.

This is the One God whose presence we remember at this midday hour. This is the One God whose mighty love conquers our hearts with a passion beyond all telling. This is the God whose Law of love is carved upon the tablets of every human heart and people. At midday, conscious of our need to open our hearts and arms to those whose cultures are different from ours, we join our Islamic sisters and brothers in praise of the One God who is Creator of all living things.

Psalm 119: 41-48

Your saving love, O God,
is like fresh water to our desert-parched lives.
Your Word is Life itself!
Give us all always your Word of Life.
Do not let us be dried up without breath.
Do not let our hearts be robbed of your presence.
Teach us always to submit to your holy will.
Give to us always your words of peace and justice.
Your path is the path of freedom.
Without you we fall into ignorance and slavery.
Place into our hearts a thirst for your law.
Let us never wander and stray from your Truth.

Your Word is our only delight.
Paradise is your garden of delights for us.
Let us worship you always and give you praise.
Glory be to God, to Christ and to the Spirit,
now and forever.
Amen.

Reading I: "The City" from the Koran
90: 1, 90: 8, 90: 20

I swear by this city (and you are a resident of this city), by the
begetter and all whom he begot. We created man to try him
with afflictions. Does he think that none has power over him?
"I have squandered vast riches," he boasts. Does he think that
none observes him? Have we not given him two eyes, a
tongue, and two lips, and shown him the two paths? Yet he
would not scale the Height. Would that you knew what
Height is. It is the freeing of a bondsman; the feeding, in the
day of famine, of an orphaned relation or a needy man in distress; to have faith and to enjoin fortitude and mercy. Those
that do this shall stand on the right hand; but those that deny
our revelations shall stand on the left, with Hell-fire close
above them.

Reading II: From *The Cost of Discipleship*,
Dietrich Bonhoeffer

"Blessed are the pure in heart: for they shall see God." Who is pure
in heart? Only those who have surrendered their hearts com-
pletely to Jesus that he may reign in them alone. Only those
whose hearts are undefiled by their own evil — and by their
own virtues too. The pure in heart have a childlike simplicity
like Adam before the fall, innocent alike of good and evil:
their hearts are not ruled by their conscience, but by the will

of Jesus. If men renounce their own good, if in penitence they have renounced their own hearts, if they rely solely upon Jesus, then his word purifies their hearts.

Purity of heart is here contrasted with all outward purity, even the purity of high intentions. The pure heart is pure alike of good and evil, it belongs exclusively to Christ and looks only to him who goes on before. Only they will see God, who in this life have looked solely unto Jesus Christ, the Son of God. For then their hearts are free from all defiling fantasies and are not distracted by conflicting desires and intentions. They are wholly absorbed by the contemplation of God. They shall see God, whose hearts have become a reflection of the image of Jesus Christ.

The Lord's Prayer (a paraphase)

Tender God,
who lives in heaven and earth,
in human reason and passion,
you are the Holy One in our midst.
Your justice is our peace;
your peace is our hope;
your presence, our delight!
Make our hands, your hands;
our hearts, your heart;
our lives, your life!
Give us this day and always
a bread of freedom to share,
a cup of hope to pour upon the earth.
Forgive us our hatreds and walls.
Teach us to forgive the walls of others as well.
Do not permit us tests beyond our strength.
And deliver us from Evil's death-grip.
For everything above us and under us,
everything within us and without us,

must bend the knee
to the Glory of your Freedom,
the everlasting Victory
of your Justice and Peace!

EVENING PRAYER

Call to Prayer

In the west, the sun is slowly sinking. From the east, the cres-
cent moon rises with a rich light to guide us into night. With
the tender warmth of a loving mother, God is stretching out
the gift of providence before us that we may know that our
lives are protected despite the temptations of the darkness. As
we come to the end of this day, we join with our sisters and
brothers in Mohammed who witness to us always the complete submission of every human heart before the loving will
of the Most High. Caught as we are in our own convictions
and beliefs, we are often blind to the presence of God in their
lives and in their hearts.

Repentant for our lack of vision, we pray this night and
always that the gentle brilliance and warm embrace of our
God would strengthen us to open our hearts to these sisters
and brothers who enrich our own communities of faith and
the community of our nation.

Evening Thanksgiving

O Loving God of every Human Heart,
from the towers of human progress
brave hearts cry out to all the earth
of the wondrous deeds of your Life and Salvation in our
    midst.
This night we offer you our evening sacrifice of praise.
This night we remember that awe-filled gift of the cross
at which our redemption was won
at the death of your Beloved.
From the darkness of this world's woes,
Jesus has led us to the bright promise of paradise

where you are ever calling us
to taste of the fresh fruit and bread of your everlasting justice
    and peace.
This night, with the People of Hagar and Ishmael,
we join and hands and hearts to give you thanks and praise.
With them we confess our sins in hope of the final day of your
    mercy.
All praise and thanks be to you, God of the evening and the
    dawn.
All praise and thanks be to you, God of every race and nation.
All praise and thanks be to you, for the gift of salvation
which is the unity of every people and faith.
All praise and honor be yours, through Christ, and the Spirit
    Wisdom,
forever and ever.
Amen.

Psalm 141

From the depths of my heart,
I cry out to you and call your name, O God.
Be not silent, but hear my pleas for your presence.
My prayers, like the smoke from incense,
go quickly up and search the crevices of the sky for you.
My hands, trembling with need, reach up and grope the air
    for you.
O God, set your seal upon my mouth.
Be the guardian of my words and, deeper, the watcher of my
    heart.
Never permit me to eat the bread of evildoers.
Never permit me — the freed slave — to put others in chains.
Make of me the instrument of your peace and forgiveness.
Let the evil strike me, I would not care.
Only keep me from walking in the way of evil.
Let my words and my prayers

FROM MANY, ONE

be a source of freedom and healing for the many.
I turn my every thought and desire to you.
You alone are my refuge.
It is you that keeps me safe in the day of evil.
Glory be to God, to Christ, and to the Spirit,
now and forever.
Amen.

Psalm 116

I was lost,
wandering as if abandoned in the desert by night.
Nothing more than the echoes of my cries to be my friend.
Only the fear-filled pulse of my heart fills the empty air.
But there is One who is near, whose ear hears my cries.
I was surrounded by the dread fears of the darkness,
like the nightmares of a child appearing on an empty wall.
Visions of fear grip my heart with sorrow and pain.
O God, deliver me from the power of night.
Then the Lord heard my cries for help, my appeals from the
    pit of despair.
This God, who is named "Compassion,"
did not leave me to sorrow and distress.
Stripped by terrors to the simplicity of my heart,
my ears heard God's cry as if new.
God protects me even in my terrors
and steals the thunder of the evening's forgetfulness.
I will turn back to rest in this Mighty One
who has kept me from the terror of the pit, the snare of death.
This is the God who wipes the tears from my eyes and makes
    my feet sure.
In the presence of the One God I will walk forever.
Glory be to God, to Christ and to the Spirit,
now and forever.
Amen.

Reading I: 1 Corinthians 13: 4-7

Love is patient; love is kind; love is not envious or boastful or
arrogant or rude. It does not insist on its own way; it is not
irritable or resentful; it does not rejoice in wrongdoing, but
rejoices in the truth. It bears all things, believes all things,
hopes all things, endures all things.

Reading II: "Night" from the Koran
92: 1, 92: 12, 92: 21

By the night, when she lets fall her darkness, and by the radiant day! By Him that created the male and the female, your
endeavors have varied ends! For him that gives in charity and
guards himself against evil and believes in goodness, We shall
smooth the path of salvation; but for him that neither gives
nor takes and disbelieves in goodness, We shall smooth the
path of affliction. When he breathes his last, his riches will not
avail him. It is for Us to give guidance. Ours is the life to
come, Ours the life of this world. I warn you, then, of the blazing fire, in which none shall burn save the hardened sinner,
who denies the Truth and gives no heed. But the good man
who purifies himself by almsgiving shall keep away from it:
and so shall he that does good works for the sake of the Most
High only, seeking no recompense. Such men shall be content.

Gospel Canticle (based on The Song of Mary)

From the depths of my very being,
my soul magnifies the goodness of our God!
God has looked upon me, a lowly servant!
For such goodness given to me,
all ages and all races will say that I am blest.
For God has done great things for me,

has given me freedom,
and raised me up into justice!
Holy is the name of the Just One!
Mercy comes from an open hand
to those who hunger for mercy's touch.
God the mighty has stretched forth an arm of love
and has lifted the lowly, scattering the proud.
God raises the downtrodden, the once powerful are no more.
God fills the starving poor, the comfortable go hungry.
God is ever mindful of the covenant with Israel,
the promise of all peace,
a promise made to Sarah, Abraham, and their children
unto the ages of ages, for every race and people.
Glory be to God, to Christ and to the Spirit,
now and forever.
Amen.

Evening Intercessions

The daylight and our labors have come to an end. The darkness of the night approaches. Yet our hearts do not fear. The brilliant lamp of our salvation in Christ is ever kindled in our midst. At this eventide, we join with the Children of Mohammed to give thanks to the One God whose presence is the salvation of all the world. Acknowledging the times we have sinned against them in hatred and discrimination, we look to a new day when the gift of human understanding will open our eyes to the presence of God fully alive in their midst. This evening we give thanks for their gifts which enrich the heritage of our nation. And so we pray: **Hear our prayers, O God of Peace.**

♦   In thanks for the gift of our Islamic sisters and brothers whose rich vision of faith widens the compassionate heart of our nation, let us pray . . .

- In thanks for the ingenuity of the Islamic peoples among us, a gift which leads us to new vistas of God's Wisdom alive in our midst, let us pray . . .

- In contrition for the times when our pride and arrogance have made us turn away from the presence of God fully alive in cultures and peoples different from ourselves, let us pray . . .

- In contrition for the hatreds and fears of other cultures which have led the human family into the horrors of war and discrimination, let us pray . . .

- For all who have died in the cause of the unity and understanding of the whole human family, especially for those from our Islamic sisters and brothers, let us pray . . .

The Lord's Prayer (a paraphase)

Tender God,
who lives in heaven and earth,
in human reason and passion,
you are the Holy One in our midst.
Your justice is our peace;
your peace is our hope;
your presence, our delight!
Make our hands, your hands;
our hearts, your heart;
our lives, your life!
Give us this day and always
a bread of freedom to share,
a cup of hope to pour upon the earth.
Forgive us our hatreds and walls.
Teach us to forgive the walls of others as well.
Do not permit us tests beyond our strength.
And deliver us from Evil's death-grip.

For everything above us and under us,
everything within us and without us,
must bend the knee
to the Glory of your Freedom,
the everlasting Victory
of your Justice and Peace!

NIGHT PRAYER

Call to Prayer

At this night hour, Jesus was taken from the cross and — dead to this world — had his body placed in the tomb waiting to be raised up to new life. Conscious how dead we are each time we take up the weaponry of hatred and bigotry, we come to the moment of sleep hopeful that God will refresh us and raise us up to a new and deeper love of every race and people and nation. At this night prayer, we pray for forgiveness and hope that the final victory of God's goodness will prevail in us and in our nation.

(Examination of Conscience)

For the bigotry that leads us to fear and hate those different than ourselves, we cry out:

Lord, have mercy.

For the times when we have been the instruments of discrimination against our Islamic sisters and brothers, we cry out:

Christ, have mercy.

For the times when our nation has closed the door of compassion to the poor , we cry out:

Lord, have mercy.

And may almighty God forgive us our sins, grace us with new life, and give us a peaceful night.

Amen.

Psalm 91

Those who dwell in the shelter of the Most High
and abide in the shadow of God's wings

say to our God, "Our refuge,
our stronghold, the God in whom we trust."
God alone frees our feet from the hunter's snare.
God hides us in the wings of freedom and love.
No shadow or arrow can frighten us.
No plague or scourge can make us fear.
Thousands may fall around us.
Yet, the faithfulness of God will protect us.
God will bear us up to heaven's height and say:
"Since you cling to me in love, I will free you.
I shall protect you for you know my name.
I shall answer whenever you call upon me.
I will save you from all distress
and I will give you glory.
With length of days I will bless you.
I shall let you taste my peace and my justice."
Glory be to God, to Christ, and to the Spirit,
now and forever.
Amen.

Reading I: 1 John 3: 11-16

For this is the message you have heard from the beginning,
that we not be like Cain who was from the evil one and mur-
dered his brother. And why did he murder him? Because his
own deeds were evil and his brother's righteous. Do not be
astonished, brothers and sisters, that the world hates you. We
know that we have passed from death to life because we love
one another. Whoever does not love abides in death. All who
hate a brother or sister are murderers, and you know that
murderers do not have eternal life abiding in them. We know
love by this, that he laid down his life for us — and we ought
to lay down our lives for one another.

Reading II: From *I Have a Dream*, Martin Luther King, Jr.

I have a dream that one day on the red hills of Georgia, sons of former slaves and sons of former slave-owners will be able to sit down together at the table of brotherhood. I have a dream that one day, even the state of Mississippi, a state sweltering with the heat of injustice, sweltering with the heat of oppression, will be transformed into an oasis of freedom and justice. I have a dream my four little children will one day live in a nation where they will not be judged by the color of their skin but by the content of their character. I have a dream today! I have a dream that one day, down in Alabama, with its vicious racists, with its governor having his lips dripping with the words of interposition and nullification, that one day, right there in Alabama, little black boys and black girls will be able to join hands with little white boys and white girls as sisters and brothers. I have a dream today! I have a dream that one day every valley shall be exalted, every hill and mountain shall be made low, the rough places shall be made plain, and the crooked places shall be made straight and the glory of the Lord will be revealed and all flesh shall see it together. This is our hope. This is the faith that I go back to the South with.

The Gospel Canticle (based on The Song of Simeon)

Now, O God of Justice,
you can dismiss your servant in the fullness of peace.
For my eyes have gazed upon the vision of your salvation,
the fulfillment of your promises of mercy
and the glory of your every race and nation.
Glory be to God, to Christ and to the Spirit,
now and forever.
Amen.

An Anthem to Mary, Mother of All the Earth

Holy Mother of all the earth,
yours are glad arms that gather the children of every nation.
You, our companion on the journey to freedom,
be with us this night and always.
As you stood faithfully near to the cross of your Child,
and held his broken body in your loving hands,
stand faithfully with us now at our many crosses.
Gather our broken lives.
Bear them to your beloved Jesus
who alone can make us one again!
O Clemens! O Pia! O Virgo Maria!
Pray for us, O Holy Mother of God,
that we may be made worthy of the promises of Christ.

Saturday

Sabbath Rest, Ever Mindful

Praying with Our Jewish American Communities

MORNING PRAYER

Call to Prayer

The sun has risen. The Sabbath-Spirit has overtaken us. We pause and rest from our labors that we might gaze with wonder upon the beauty of creation and the gift of our presence to one another in love and compassion. On this day of grace, we join our lives with the Children of Sarah and Abraham, our Jewish sisters and brothers in the faith. We give God praise and adoration for the presence of the Spirit in our common ancestors — a Spirit that gave them the courage to leave comforts and home for a land of promise, there to do God's will.

We remember with joy the bestowal of the law on Sinai's height. Ringing in our ears are the words of the prophets ever calling us back to that original covenant which is carved deep within us and pulses through our veins. On this day of Sabbath rest, keeping before our eyes the incomprehensible horror of a Holocaust never to be forgotten, we join with our Jewish American communities to pray for an end to every scandalous human bigotry that slaps the face of this nation's promise of justice and equality for all.

Morning Praise

Ancient of Days,
as morning dawns we raise our voices in adoration.
On the seventh day, you rested from the labor of creation
looking upon the works of your hands, pronouncing them as
   "good."
On this day of Sabbath rest, we join our hearts and lives
with our ancestors in the faith:
the Children of Sarah and Abraham
whose tenacity of spirit and joy of life
give them the strength to be guardians of your covenant.
Ever called to the deepest recesses of your Holy Heart,

our Jewish sisters and brothers give brilliant witness
to the beauty of your Law, the bond of your love and peace.
You are no God who loves evil, who despises the death of
    your people.
Rather you call us to tend the goodness of creation
to make this earth a home for all living things.
In the fullness of time, you called our sisters and brothers
from the slavery of Egypt to the liberty of a promised land.
Into this present age, through the death of Jesus,
you continue to call all creation from the slavery of sin
to the freedom of unbounded life in you!
All praise and honor be yours, through Christ and the Spirit
    Wisdom,
forever and ever.
Amen.

Psalm 63

My soul is thirsty for you, O God.
Like a desert for water, I hunger for your love.
I look for you in the sanctuaries of the earth,
in all the secret recesses of the human heart.
More precious than bread and life is your love, your touch.
New to this day, my dry mouth gives you thirsty praise.
Every sinew and fiber of my body is filled with longing for
    your presence.
I give you praise.
I lift up my hands to you and bless your holy name.
Look toward me. Fill me with the banquet of your loving.
Make my mouth speak words of praise to you.
All through the empty night, through my tears of loneliness,
I long for your touch, your gentle presence.
Your presence invades my every thought and dream.
You are my help. I delight under the shadow of your love.
Like one who has fallen, I cling to you for my life.
You catch me and lift me up to safety.

Glory be to God, to Christ and to the Spirit,
now and forever.
Amen.

Psalm 92

With the sound of many instruments,
we give thanks to the Most High God.
It is ever good to give thanks and praise to God
whose strains of love echo in our hearts and minds
and make our feet to dance.
What choice have we but to proclaim the love of God each
morning?
Your deeds place laughter in our hearts
and merriment in our throats.
No one can ever plumb the depths of your holy will.
Evil is no path for your people. It has no final joy.
The works of the evil die like withered grass in a wild garden.
But the just ones you make like a strong tree
towering over the field and green with life.
Rooted in your house, your Just Tree gives shade and joy to
human hearts.
We flourish in the court of the world, O God.
We proclaim your justice and sing of your mighty deeds of
salvation.
You are our Foundation and our Liberty.
To you be adoration forever!
Glory be to God, to Christ, and to the Spirit,
now and forever.
Amen.

Reading I: Exodus 14: 26-31

Then the LORD said to Moses, "Stretch out your hand over the
sea, so that the water may come back upon the Egyptians,
upon their chariots and chariot drivers." So Moses stretched

out his hand over the sea, and at dawn the sea returned to its normal depth. As the Egyptians fled before it, the LORD tossed the Egyptians into the sea. The waters returned and covered the chariots and the chariot drivers, the entire army of Pharaoh that had followed them into the sea; not one of them remained. But the Israelites walked on dry ground through the sea, the waters forming a wall for them on their right and on their left. Thus the LORD saved Israel that day from the Egyptians; and Israel saw the Egyptians dead on the seashore. Israel saw the great work that the LORD did against the Egyptians. So the people feared the LORD and believed in the LORD and in his servant Moses.

Reading II: Meditation #8 from *Gates of Prayer for Weekdays*

Prayer is speech, but not 'mere' speech. The word is not to be despised. Words have power over the soul. "Hear, O Israel!" is a cry and an affirmation, a reminder of glory and martyrdom, a part of the very essence of our people's history. Our prayer books are but words on paper; they can mean little or nothing. Yet the searching spirit and questing heart may find great power in their words. Through them we link ourselves to all the generations of our people, pouring out our souls in prayer with those of our brothers and sisters. These words, laden with the tears and joys of centuries, have the power to bring us into the very presence of God. Not easily, not all at once, not every time, but somehow, sometimes, the worshipper who offers up heart and mind without reservation will know that she has touched the Throne of Glory.

Gospel Canticle (based on The Song of Zechariah)

Blessed may you be, O God of Israel, our Redeemer!
Blessed is your everlasting love
which hungers for our freedom!

Blessed may you be for sending us a Savior
from the Holy House of David!
From the mouths of wandering prophets
your ancient promise of liberty was spoken.
You promised to deliver us, to save us from our enemies,
and all who wish us hatred.
You remember your covenant of peace
having sworn to set us free, to break our chains:
free to live upon this earth without fear
all the days of our lives.
O newborn child, you shall be the prophet of the Lord!
You shall go before God's presence with words of promise.
You shall bring the brightness of salvation and peace;
and announce the tender mercy of God like a dawn
to all who dwell in darkness and the shadow of death,
guiding our feet into the pathways of all peace.
Glory be to God, to Christ and to the Spirit,
now and forever.
Amen.

Acclamations of Praise

On this Sabbath, joined with our Jewish sisters and brothers,
we acclaim the Holy One of Israel who suffers with his people
and daily breathes the Spirit of Freedom within us as we pray:
Holy One, all praise be yours.

♦   We worship the God who called our ancestors in the faith
    to a covenant of lasting peace for all the world as we
    pray . . .

♦   We praise the God who rescued Israel from the bondage
    of oppression and slavery, and led them to the freedom of
    the promise as we pray . . .

♦ We are filled with wonder at the presence of God whose
  Spirit in our hearts shatters the chains of human bigotry
  and oppression which enslave so many as we pray . . .

♦ We give praise and honor to the God of Sarah and
  Abraham who mourns loudly every human holocaust and
  desires only the sacrifice of love and mercy as we pray . . .

The Lord's Prayer (a paraphase)

Tender God,
who lives in heaven and earth,
in human reason and passion,
you are the Holy One in our midst.
Your justice is our peace;
your peace is our hope;
your presence, our delight!
Make our hands, your hands;
our hearts, your heart;
our lives, your life!
Give us this day and always
a bread of freedom to share,
a cup of hope to pour upon the earth.
Forgive us our hatreds and walls.
Teach us to forgive the walls of others as well.
Do not permit us tests beyond our strength.
And deliver us from Evil's death-grip.
For everything above us and under us,
everything within us and without us,
must bend the knee
to the Glory of your Freedom,
the everlasting Victory
of your Justice and Peace!

MIDDAY PRAYER

Call to Prayer

Midway through this day of Sabbath rest, we pause to
remember in prayer the presence of the Holy One whose
majesty is displayed in all the works of creation. Together
with the Children of Sarah and Abraham, our sisters and
brothers in the faith, we call to mind the saving promise of
our common gift of salvation. Saddened by the evil which
leads human hearts and human nations to discriminate
against the innocent, we remember the call of God who bids
us repent by welcoming the stranger, tending the hungers of
the poor, and breaking the chains of all in slavery.
At this midday hour, we remember that God makes the sun
and the rain to shine and fall upon every living being without
discrimination. Our God gives equally to every woman, man,
and child. There is no favoritism in God. The sole favor of
God is the one law of love, enjoined upon us equally. We pray
fervently that God would set us free from our hatreds and
bigotry. We pray for a resurgence of the covenant among us
all that we may announce a jubilee of freedom to every people
and nation.

Psalm 119: 49-56

O God, you remember us in our many needs.
This day, we remember as well.
We remember your words of promise to us from long ago.
In the heat of our labors, they are our refreshment and joy.
Your Word, your Law, we remember with hope.
Your presence is our comfort in times of sorrow;
like the noonday sun, lighting our way toward evening.
Breathe forth your Spirit upon us, O God.

Strengthen us for the works of your gift of salvation.
Always it seems we are utterly derided
for clinging to your words that give us life.
The wicked laugh at us and mock us. They scorn our devotion
to your Law.
Here in our exile our gentle song rises above the mockery of
the crowd.
We think of you all the day and night long
hoping for the final victory of your promises to us.
Bless us always with your strength
that we may bear your presence to all peoples
and thus announce your blessing to the nations.
Glory be to God, to Christ and to the Spirit,
now and forever.
Amen.

Reading I: "Hear O Israel", from *Jacob the Baker* by Noah Ben Shea

Throughout the day, long lines stretched in the bakery, hoping to make contact with Jacob. Jacob, for his part, didn't seem sure what to make of this attention. In fact, he didn't seem interested in making anything of it. A man, whose facial muscles jumped as he spoke, pushed toward Jacob and in a nervous half-whisper said: "Jacob! I keep hearing a voice calling out my name." "But why does this make you uncomfortable?" asked Jacob. "Because it is my voice," said the man. Jacob took the man's hands and pressed them between his own. "We should only be frightened when we cannot hear ourselves. Often we create our own deafness and then grow so familiar with our deafness that the thought of hearing becomes frightening."

Reading II: from *The Cost of Discipleship,* Dietrich Bonhoeffer

"Blessed are the peacemakers, for they shall be called the children of God." The followers of Jesus have been called to peace. When he called them they found their peace, for he is their peace. But now they are told they must not only *have* peace but m a k e it. And to that end they renounce all violence and tumult. In the cause of Christ nothing is to be gained by such methods. His kingdom is one of peace, and the mutual greeting of his flock is a greeting of peace. His disciples keep the peace by choosing to endure suffering themselves rather than inflict it on others. They maintain fellowship when others would break it off. They renounce all self-assertion, and quietly suffer in the face of hatred and wrong. In so doing they overcome evil with good, and establish the peace of God in a world of war and hate.

"Blessed are they that have been persecuted for righteousness' sake: for theirs is the kingdom of heaven." This does not refer to the righteousness of God, but to suffering in a just cause, suffering for their own just judgments and actions. For it is by these that they who renounce possessions, fortune, rights, righteousness, honor, and force for the sake of following Christ, will be distinguished from the world. The world will be offended at them, and so the disciples will be persecuted for righteousness' sake. Not recognition, but rejection, is the reward they get from the world for their message and works. It is important that Jesus gives his blessing not merely to suffering incurred directly for the confession of his name, but to suffering in any just cause. They receive the same promise as the poor, for in persecution they are equals in poverty.

The Lord's Prayer (a paraphase)

Tender God,
who lives in heaven and earth,
in human reason and passion,
you are the Holy One in our midst.
Your justice is our peace;
your peace is our hope;
your presence, our delight!
Make our hands, your hands;
our hearts, your heart;
our lives, your life!
Give us this day and always
a bread of freedom to share,
a cup of hope to pour upon the earth.
Forgive us our hatreds and walls.
Teach us to forgive the walls of others as well.
Do not permit us tests beyond our strength.
And deliver us from Evil's death-grip.
For everything above us and under us,
everything within us and without us,
must bend the knee
to the Glory of your Freedom,
the everlasting Victory
of your Justice and Peace!

EVENING PRAYER

Call to Prayer

Evening has descended upon us. The last lights of this
Sabbath day have been kindled. In the coming darkness, the
light of hope within our hearts is set on fire once again. With
our Jewish sisters and brothers, we are called to remember.
This is not a dead memory of things long past and no longer
pulsing in our veins. Our remembering is a living sense of
memory that keeps alive the awe-filled power of a God who
dares, against the angry protests of the mighty, to set captives
free and raise up the poor to the dignity of princes.

At this eventide, filled with praise and thanksgiving for
the rich gifts from every race which grace our one nation, we
are filled likewise with a spirit of sincere repentance for the
horrors and atrocities which human ignorance has visited
upon all those we deem different than ourselves. With what
majesty God calls us to a continual conversion of life! With
what gentle might does the Maker of Heaven and Earth
remind us that every woman, man, and child is the tabernacle, the ark, of the divine presence. This night, like a flame
blazing once again, the bright vision of the unity of all creation is set before us to light up the darkness that too often
haunts our lives. With Christ Jesus, the Lamp of God's Justice,
we offer this evening sacrifice of praise and thanks.

Evening Thanksgiving

Great Ruler of the Universe,
Mighty God who puts to flight the terrors of the night,
all praise and thanks be yours

through Christ who is your Beloved Child.
Evening is descending upon us.
The incense of our repentant prayers is raised before you.
Despite the terrors of the coming darkness, you do not leave
us as orphans.
Rather you kindle in our midst the Brilliant Flame of your
Justice
which leaps up from the heart of your Beloved
and gives warm hope to all those who have been ravaged by
human hatred.
This night we join our lives with the Children of Sarah and
Abraham.
The memory of your wonderful deeds unites us with them in
the one faith.
With them we grieve for the inhumanity of the nations
which led them to slavery and thereby enslaved the hope of
all the world.
As evening falls upon us, we proclaim that your liberty
descends on us as well
breaking the chains of despair and strengthening our limbs
and hearts
to break the shackles of human ignorance and hatred.
All praise and thanks to you, O Sabbath Lord and God of
Justice!
All praise and thanks to you, O God who leads us from the
darkness of slavery
into the brilliant promise of that final day
when the victory of Christ shall bring all the nations
into the wondrous and final light of your peace!
All praise and honor be yours, through Christ and the Spirit
Wisdom,
forever and ever.
Amen.

FROM MANY, ONE

Psalm 141

From the depths of my heart,
I cry out to you and call your name, O God.
Be not silent, but hear my pleas for your presence.
My prayers, like the smoke from incense,
go quickly up and search the crevices of the sky for you.
My hands, trembling with need, reach up and grope the air
    for you.
O God, set your seal upon my mouth.
Be the guardian of my words and, deeper, the watcher of my
    heart.
Never permit me to eat the bread of evildoers.
Never permit me —- the freed slave —- to put others in
    chains.
Make of me the instrument of your peace and forgiveness.
Let the evil strike me, I would not care.
Only keep me from walking in the way of evil.
Let my words and my prayers
be a source of freedom and healing for the many.
I turn my every thought and desire to you.
You alone are my refuge.
It is you that keeps me safe in the day of evil.
Glory be to God, to Christ, and to the Spirit,
now and forever.
Amen.

Psalm 113

From the rising of the sun to its setting,
the praise of God echoes from the seas and the nations.
From east to west, a perfect sacrifice of praise we offer!
All servants of God in all the nations.
Proclaim the God whose word is Justice,
whose name means Peace!

Bless the God of our ancestors both now and forevermore!
God indeed is above the heavens and the earth.
The ways of God are beyond the limits of our minds and
    hearts.
There can be none to compare with the Justice of God,
with the Peace of God which is our only hope.
God never leaves us in our distress.
Even in seeming silence, there is the Presence of God
who breathes and grieves with us in our sorrows.
Like a hand in glove, God lives, walks among us
seeing us in our every need.
God will raise the poor and the lowly.
God will bring down the mighty and the arrogant from their
    thrones.
God will fill the hungry and give freedom to the captive.
God will make the sterile to leap in fruitful joy!
Praise, all servants of the Lord,
the God who gives glad tidings of love to the families of
    nations.
Glory be to God, to Christ, and to the Spirit,
now and forever.
Amen.

Reading I: 1 Corinthians 13: 8-13

Love never ends. But as for prophecies, they will come to an
end; as for tongues, they will cease; as for knowledge, it will
come to an end. For we know only in part, and we prophesy
only in part, but when the complete comes, the partial will
come to an end. When I was a child, I spoke like a child, I
thought like a child, I reasoned like a child; when I became an
adult, I put an end to childish ways. For now we see in a mir-
ror, dimly, but then we shall see face to face. Now I know only
in part; then I will know fully even as I have been fully

known. And now faith, hope and love abide, these three; and the greatest of these is love.

Reading II: "Our Martyrs," Mourners Kaddish #13 from *Gates of Prayer for Weekdays*

We have lived in numberless towns and villages; and in too many of them we have endured cruel suffering. Some we have forgotten; others are sealed into our memory, a wound that does not heal. A hundred generations of victims and martyrs; still their blood cries out from the earth. And so many, so many at Dachau, at Buchenwald, at Babi Yar, and . . . What can we say? What can we do? How bear the unbearable, or accept what life has brought to our people? All who are born must die, but how shall we compare the slow passage of our days with the callous slaughter of the innocent, cut off before their time? They lived with faith. Not all, but many. And, surely, many died with faith; faith in God, in life, in the goodness that even flames cannot destroy. May we find a way to the strength of that faith, that trust, that sure sense that life and soul endure beyond this body's death.

Gospel Canticle (based on The Song of Mary)

From the depths of my very being,
my soul magnifies the goodness of our God!
God has looked upon me, a lowly servant!
For such goodness given to me,
all ages and all races will say that I am blest.
For God has done great things for me,
has given me freedom,
and raised me up into justice!
Holy is the name of the Just One!
Mercy comes from an open hand

to those who hunger for mercy's touch.
God the mighty has stretched forth an arm of love
and has lifted the lowly, scattering the proud.
God raises the downtrodden, the once powerful are no more.
God fills the starving poor, the comfortable go hungry.
God is ever mindful of the covenant with Israel,
the promise of all peace,
a promise made to Sarah, Abraham, and their children
unto the ages of ages, for every race and people.
Glory be to God, to Christ and to the Spirit,
now and forever.
Amen.

Evening Intercessions

We have come to end of this Sabbath. The sun is setting and evening is upon us. As we journey into night's beginning, we join with our Jewish sisters and brothers to celebrate our common heritage in Sarah and Abraham. Remembering the horrors of the Holocaust, we pray in a particular way this night, in communion with that brave mother who held the dead Christ, for an end to discrimination and bigotry in our nation and throughout the world. We pray for the coming of a New Dawn of Justice for every living thing. Repentant yet hopeful of God's final victory in Christ, we offer our prayers to the God who knows our needs before we ask. And so we pray: **Gracious God, accept our prayer.**

◆ In thanks for the heritage and gifts of our Jewish sisters and brothers, our special friends in the heritage of faith, let us pray . . .

◆ In thanks for the spirit of freedom and justice which this nation claims as its heritage, and which the poor and the victimized claim as their human right, let us pray . . .

◆ In contrition for the horror of the Holocaust, that we might ever remember the depravity to which human hearts and nations can sink in their selfishness, let us pray . . .

◆ In contrition for the greed, avarice, and political lusts for power in our midst, that these weapons of destruction which taunt the defenseless might be abolished from our lives, let us pray . . .

◆ For all who have died as the victims of human hatred, for all those who have given their lives for justice and peace, in a special way for the victims of the Holocaust, that the deaths of all these faithful may not go unredeemed, let us pray . . .

The Lord's Prayer (a paraphase)

Tender God,
who lives in heaven and earth,
in human reason and passion,
you are the Holy One in our midst.
Your justice is our peace;
your peace is our hope;
your presence, our delight!
Make our hands, your hands;
our hearts, your heart;
our lives, your life!
Give us this day and always
a bread of freedom to share,
a cup of hope to pour upon the earth.
Forgive us our hatreds and walls.
Teach us to forgive the walls of others as well.
Do not permit us tests beyond our strength.
And deliver us from Evil's death-grip.
For everything above us and under us,

everything within us and without us,
must bend the knee
to the Glory of your Freedom,
the everlasting Victory
of your Justice and Peace!

NIGHT PRAYER

Call to Prayer

Day has come to an end. Before the gift of sleep shuts our eyes and we sink into refreshment, we come to prayer with our Jewish sisters and brothers. As we enter this moment, we ask for the grace of the Holy Spirit to shed the divine light upon us that we may know our sins and be bathed with the gift of sincere and uncompromising repentance.

(Examination of Conscience)

For the horror of the Holocaust the memory of which can inspire us to a deeper justice, we cry out:

Lord, have mercy.

For the times when our individual selfishness has led us to victimize others, we cry out:

Christ, have mercy.

For the times when our nation has become deaf and blind to the needs of the many who make up the unity of America, we cry out:

Lord, have mercy.

And may almighty God forgive us our sins, grace us with new life, and give us a peaceful night.

Amen.

Psalm 91

Those who dwell in the shelter of the Most High
and abide in the shadow of God's wings
say to our God, "Our refuge,
our stronghold, the God in whom we trust."

God alone frees our feet from the hunter's snare.
God hides us in the wings of freedom and love.
No shadow or arrow can frighten us.
No plague or scourge can make us fear.
Thousands may fall around us.
Yet, the faithfulness of God will protect us.
God will bear us up to heaven's height and say:
"Since you cling to me in love, I will free you.
I shall protect you for you know my name.
I shall answer whenever you call upon me.
I will save you from all distress
and I will give you glory.
With length of days I will bless you.
I shall let you taste my peace and my justice."
Glory be to God, to Christ and to the Spirit,
now and forever.
Amen.

Reading I: 1 John 4: 7-11

Beloved, let us love one another, because love is from God; everyone who loves is born of God and knows God. Whoever does not love does not know God, for God is love. God's love was revealed among us in this way: God sent his only Son into the world so that we might live through him. In this is love, not that we loved God but that he loved us and sent his Son to be the atoning sacrifice for our sins. Beloved, since God loved us so much. we also ought to love one another.

Reading II: From *I Have a Dream*, Martin Luther King, Jr.

With this faith we will be able to hear out of the mountain of despair a stone of hope. With this faith we will be able to transform the jangling discords of our nation into a beautiful symphony of brotherhood. With this faith we will be able to work together, to pray together, to struggle together, to hail together, to stand up for freedom together, knowing that we will be free one day. This will be the day when all of God's children will be able to sing with new meaning — "my country 'tis of thee; sweet land of liberty; of thee I sing; land where my fathers died, land of the pilgrim's pride; from every mountain side, let freedom ring" — and if America is to be a great nation, this must become true.

So let freedom ring from the prodigious hilltops of New Hampshire. Let freedom ring from the mighty mountains of New York. Let freedom ring from the heightening Alleghenies of Pennsylvania. Let freedom ring from the snowcapped Rockies of Colorado. Let freedom ring from the curvaceous slopes of California. But not only that. Let freedom ring from the Stone Mountain of Georgia. Let freedom ring from Lookout Mountain of Tennessee. Let freedom ring from every hill and molehill of Mississippi, from every mountainside, let freedom ring.

And when we allow freedom to ring, when we let it ring from every village and hamlet, from every state and city, we will be able to speed up that day when all of God's children — black men and white men, Jews and Gentiles, Catholics and Protestants — will be able to join hands and to sing in the words of the old Negro spiritual, "Free at last, free at last; thank God Almighty, we are free at last."

The Gospel Canticle (based on The Song of Simeon)

Now, O God of Justice,
you can dismiss your servant in the fullness of peace.
For my eyes have gazed upon the vision of your salvation,
the fulfillment of your promises of mercy
and the glory of your every race and nation.
Glory be to God, to Christ and to the Spirit,
now and forever.
Amen.

An Anthem to Mary, Mother of All the Earth

Holy Mother of all the earth,
yours are glad arms that gather the children of every nation.
You, our companion on the journey to freedom,
be with us this night and always.
As you stood faithfully near to the cross of your Child,
and held his broken body in your loving hands,
stand faithfully with us now at our many crosses.
Gather our broken lives.
Bear them to your beloved Jesus
who alone can make us one again!
O Clemens! O Pia! O Virgo Maria!
Pray for us, O Holy Mother of God,
that we may be made worthy of the promises of Christ.

Acknowledgements:

All psalm-poems and canticle-poems are the author's own compositions. Other biblical passages are taken from *The New Revised Standard Version,* copyright © 1989 Division of Christian Education of the National Council of Churches in the U.S.A.

Excerpts from the Documents of Vatican II are from Vatican II: *The Conciliar and Post Conciliar Documents,* Austin Flannery, O.P., General Editor, copyright © 1975 by Costello Publishing Company and Austin Flannery.

Selections from *The Cost of Discipleship* by Dietrich Bonhoeffer, translated from the German by R.H. Fuller, with some revision by Irmgard Booth. Copyright © 1959 by SCM Press, Ltd. Reprinted with the permission of Simon & Schuster, Inc.

Reprinted by arrangement with the Heirs to the Estate of Martin Luther King, Jr., c/o Joan Davies Agency as agent for the Proprietor: Copyright © 1963 by Martin Luther King, Jr., copyright renewed 1991 by Coretta Scott King. "I Have a Dream." Copyright © 1967 by Martin Luther King, Jr. "A Christmas Sermon on Peace."

Copyright ownership for *Untitled* by Ana Iras Varas cound not be found. It is taken from *From The Republic of Conscience: An International Anthology of Poetry,* Kerry Flattley and Chris Wallace-Crabbe, Editors, White Pine Press, Fredonia, New York, copyright © 1992 Kerry Flattley and Chris Wallace-Crabbe with Aird Books and Amnesty International.

"The God of Children" by Margorie Agosin from *Zones of Pain* translated by Cola Franzen, Fredonia , New York: White Pine Press, copyright © 1988, p. 18.

"A Story" by Robert Saballos from *On the Front Line: Guerilla Poems of El Salvador,* edited and translated by Claribel Alegria and Darwin J. Flakoll, (Curbstone Press, 1989). Translation copyright © 1989 by Claribel Alegria and Darwin J. Flakoll. Reprinted with permission of Curbstone Press. Distributed by InBook.

"Question and Answer" from *The Panther and the Lash,* by Langston Hughes. Copyright © 1967 by Langston Hughes Reprinted by permission of Alfred A. Knopf, Inc.